Basílíkon Doron
The King's Gift

Basilikon Doron
The King's Gift

King James Stuart

Creative Minority Productions
Montrose, CA

Contents

Introduction

James Stuart—King James VI of Scotland—wrote *Basilikon Doron* ("Kingly Gift") for his then six-year-old son, Henry. The book was meant to distill all of James' knowledge about king-craft, both practical and theoretical, into a brief primer. In 1599 the *Doron* was finished and James had seven copies printed, which he entrusted to a small circle of reliable servants to be given to Henry when he was old enough, even if James did not survive so long—a reasonable precaution, given the short average lifespans of Elizabethan men, particularly those involved in politics.

At least one of these copies was leaked—by accident or artifice—and pirate editions began appearing, prompting James to release an authorized edition in 1603...the same year he traveled to London to take the throne of England. A French edition (purged of the worst of its pro-protestant rhetoric) followed.

Unfortunately the originally intended audience, Prince Henry, died in 1616, before he could inherit his father's thrones. Generations of readers have, however, benefited from reading the book. This edition acknowledges the fact that fewer readers than in James' day are proficient in Latin nor versed in classical allusions and seeks to provide sufficient annotations to keep the work accessible to a twenty-first century audience.

Biographical Notes

JAMES I. (1566–1625),[1] king of Great Britain and Ireland, and king of Scotland as James VI., was the only child of Mary Queen of Scots and her second husband, Henry Stewart Lord Darnley. He was born in the castle of Edinburgh on the 19th of June, 1566, and was proclaimed king of Scotland on the 24th of July, 1567, upon the forced abdication of his mother. Until 1578 he was treated as being incapable of taking any real part in public affairs, and was kept in the castle of Stirling for safety's sake amid the confused fighting of the early years of his minority.

The king was physically fragile as a boy. It is said that he could not stand without support until he was seven and, although he lived until he was nearly sixty, he was never a strong man. In later life he was a constant and even a reckless rider, but the weakness in his legs was never quite cured; for most of his life he had to be tied to the saddle. When, on one occasion in 1621, his horse threw him into the New River near his favorite palace of Theobalds in the neighborhood of London, he narrowly escaped being drowned; yet he continued to ride as before. At all times he preferred to lean on the shoulder of an attendant when walking. This feebleness of body was attributed to the agitations and the violent efforts forced on his mother by the murder of her secretary Rizzio when she was in the sixth month of her pregnancy. The fact that James

---

[1]Part of this essay was printed previously in *The Encyclopaedia Britannica,* 11th ed.

Genealogy of James I/VI

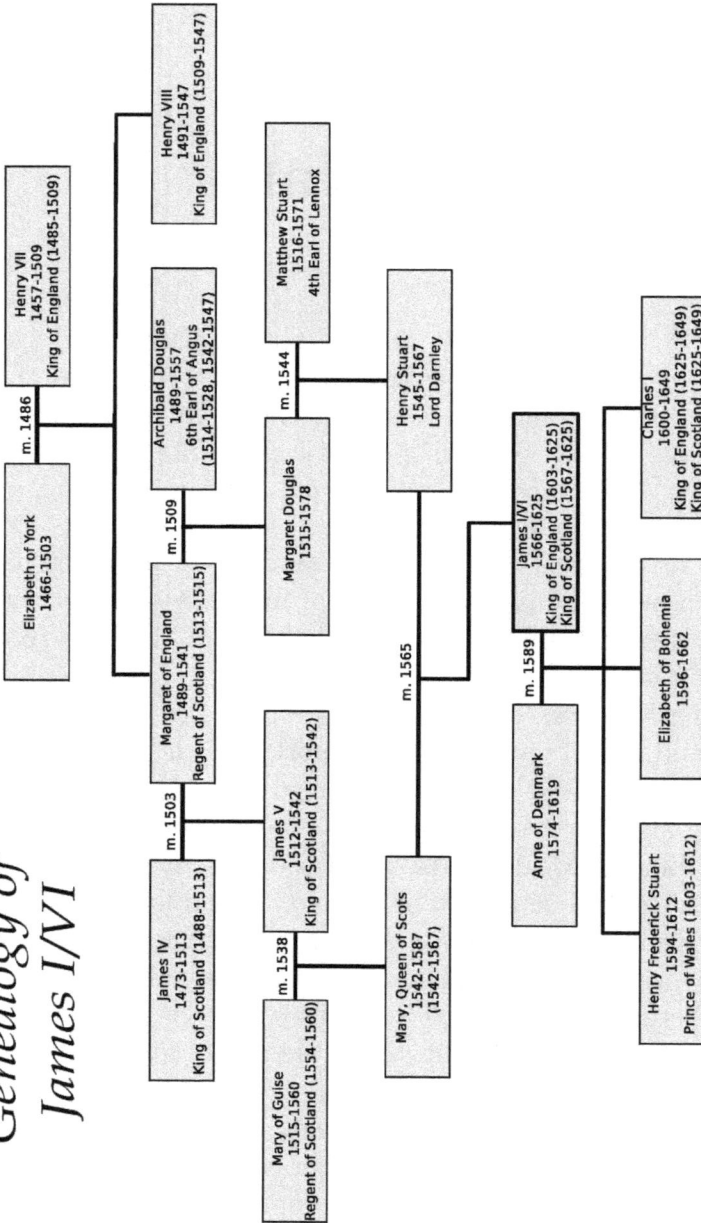

Henry VII
1457-1509
King of England (1485-1509)

Elizabeth of York
1466-1503

m. 1486

Henry VIII
1491-1547
King of England (1509-1547)

Archibald Douglas
1489-1557
6th Earl of Angus
(1514-1528, 1542-1547)

Matthew Stuart
1516-1571
4th Earl of Lennox

m. 1509

Margaret of England
1489-1541
Regent of Scotland (1513-1515)

Margaret Douglas
1515-1578

m. 1544

Henry Stuart
1545-1567
Lord Darnley

James IV
1473-1513
King of Scotland (1488-1513)

m. 1503

James V
1512-1542
King of Scotland (1513-1542)

Mary of Guise
1515-1560
Regent of Scotland (1554-1560)

m. 1538

Mary, Queen of Scots
1542-1587
(1542-1567)

m. 1565

James I/VI
1566-1625
King of England (1603-1625)
King of Scotland (1567-1625)

Anne of Denmark
1574-1619

m. 1589

Charles I
1600-1649
King of England (1625-1649)
King of Scotland (1625-1649)

Elizabeth of Bohemia
1596-1662

Henry Frederick Stuart
1594-1612
Prince of Wales (1603-1612)

was a bold rider, in spite of this serious disqualification for athletic exercise, should be borne in mind when he is accused of having been a coward.

The circumstances surrounding him in boyhood were not favorable to the development of his character. His immediate guardian or foster father, the Earl of Mar, was indeed an honorable man, and the countess, who had charge of the nursing of the king, discharged her duty so as to win his lasting confidence. James later entrusted her with the care of his eldest son, Henry. When the earl died in 1572 his place was well filled by his brother, Sir Alexander Erskine. The king's education was placed under the care of George Buchanan, assisted by Peter Young, and two other tutors. Buchanan, who did not spare the rod, and the other teachers, who had more reverence for the royal person, gave the boy a sound training in languages and Protestant theology. The quality of his education helped to give him a taste for learning, but also a tendency towards pedantry.

James was only twelve when the earl of Morton was driven from the regency, and for some time after he can have been no more than a puppet in the hands of intriguers and party leaders. When, for instance, in 1582 he was seized by the faction of nobles who carried out the so-called raid of Ruthven, which was in fact a kidnapping enterprise carried out in the interest of the Protestant party, he cried like a child. One of the conspirators, the master of Glamis, Sir Thomas Lyon, told him that it was better "bairns should greet [children should cry] than bearded men."[2] It was not indeed till 1583, when he broke away from his captors, that James began to govern in reality.

James's work as a ruler can be divided into black and white—into the part which was a failure and a preparation for future disaster, and the part which was solid achievement, honorable to himself and profitable to his people. His native

---

[2]James was then 16 years old.

kingdom of Scotland had the benefit of the second. Between 1583 and 1603 he reduced the anarchical baronage of Scotland to obedience, and replaced the subdivision of sovereignty and consequent confusion, which had been the very essence of feudalism, by a strong centralized royal authority. In fact he did in Scotland the work which had been done by the Tudors in England, by Louis XI in France, and by Ferdinand and Isabella in Spain. It was the work of all the strong rulers of the Renaissance. But James not only brought his disobedient and intriguing barons to order—that was a comparatively easy achievement and might well have been performed by more than one of his predecessors, had their lives been prolonged— he also quelled the attempts of the Protestants to found what has been called a "Presbyterian Hildebrandism" by enforcing the superiority of the state over the church. Both before his accession to the throne of England (1603) and afterwords he took an intelligent interest in the prosperity of his Scottish kingdom, and did much for the pacification of the Hebrides, for the enforcement of order on the Borders, and for the development of industry. That he did so much although the crown was poor (largely it must be confessed because he made profuse gifts of the secularized church lands), and although the armed force at his disposal was so small that to the very end he was exposed to the attacks of would-be kidnappers (as in the case of the Gowrie conspiracy of 1600), is proof positive that he was neither the mere poltroon nor the mere learned fool he has often been called.

James's methods of achieving ends in themselves honorable and profitable were indeed of a kind which has made posterity unjust to his real merits. The circumstances in which he passed his youth developed in him a natural tendency to craft. He boasted indeed of his "king-craft" and probably believed that he owed it to his studies. But it was in reality the resource of the weak, the art of playing off one possible enemy against another by trickery, and so deceiving all. The Marquis de Fontenay, the French ambassador, who saw him in the early part of his reign, speaks of him as cowed by the violence about him. It is certain that James was most unscrupulous in making promises which he never meant to keep, and the terror in which he passed his youth sufficiently explains his preference for guile. He would make promises to everybody, as when he wrote to the pope in 1584 more than hinting that he would be a good Roman Catholic if helped in his need. His very natural desire to escape from the poverty and insecurity of Scotland to the opulent English throne not only kept him busy in intrigues to placate the Roman Catholics or anybody else who could help or hinder him, but led him to behave basely in regard to the execution of his mother in 1587. He blustered to give himself an air of courage, but took good care to do nothing to offend Elizabeth. When the time came for fulfilling his promises and half-promises, he was not able, even if he had been willing, to keep his word to everybody. The methods which had helped him to success in Scotland did him harm in England, where his reign prepared the way for the great civil war. Although England accepted him as the alternative to civil war, and although he was received and surrounded with fulsome flattery, he never won the respect of his English subjects. His undignified personal appearance was against him, and so were his garrulity, his Scottish accent, his slovenliness and his toleration of disorders in his court, but, above all, his favor for handsome male favorites, whom he loaded with gifts and caressed with demonstrations of affection which laid him open to suspicions of homosexuality. In ecclesiastical matters he offended many, who contrasted his severity and rudeness to the Puritan divines at the Hampton Court Conference[3] with his politeness to the Roman Catholics, whom he, however,

---

[3]James always viewed the Puritan faction as dangerous extremists and was loath to grant concessions that would stand as precedents. The Hampton Court Conference (1604) resulted in several minor doctrinal compromises, including the decision to commission a new denomination-neutral "Authorized Version" of the Bible which came to be known in later years as the "King James" version.

worried by fits and starts. In a country where the authority of the state had been firmly established and the problem was how to keep it from degenerating into the mere instrument of a king's passions, his insistence on the doctrine of divine right aroused distrust and hostility. In itself, and in its origin, the doctrine was nothing more than a necessary assertion of the independence of the state in face of the "Hildebrandism" of Rome and Geneva alike. But when Englishmen were told that the king alone had indefeasible rights, and that all the privileges of subjects were revocable gifts, they were roused to hostility. His weaknesses cast suspicion on his best meant schemes. His favor for his countrymen helped to defeat his wise wish to bring about a full union between England and Scotland. His profusion, which had been bad in the poverty of Scotland and was boundless amid the wealth of England, kept him starved for liquid assets, and drove him to shifts. Posterity can give him credit for his desire to forward religious peace in Europe, but his Protestant subjects were simply frightened when he sought a matrimonial alliance with Spain. Sagacious men among his contemporaries could not see the consistency of a king who married his daughter Elizabeth to the elector palatine, a leader of the German Protestants, and also sought to marry his son to an infanta of Spain. The king's subservience to Spain was indeed almost besotted. He could not see her real weakness, and he allowed himself to be fooled by the ministers of Philip III and Philip IV. The end of his scheming was that he was dragged into a needless war with Spain by his son Charles and his favorite George Villiers, Duke of Buckingham, just before his death on the 5th of March 1625 at Theobalds.

Over the centuries, many historians have painted James I/VI as a weakling or a fool. Certainly, his reign had its failures: he allowed England's once preeminent navy to decline to insignificance, allowed the country to become entangled in the opening stages conflict which we now know as the Thirty Years Wars, and allowed social and religious tensions to build which, after his death, lead directly to the English Civil War.

A kinder picture, however, shows us a man who genuinely meant well and tried to do his duty, but was sometimes unequal to the job. James was a portly, good-natured man of only average intelligence who avoided conflict and was happiest when watching plays or reading old books. He would have excelled as a country squire or a grammar school teacher, but was instead required to secede one of the most charismatic and skillful monarchs in European history. James was only a mediocre King, but even an above-average ruler would have made a poor showing in comparison to Elizabeth.

True, James' trusting nature made him too ready to promote handsome young favorites above the level of their competence, and too slow to recognize or censure intrigue in his court. But he was— particularly by the standards of the age— a moral man. If anything his main failing was that he lacked the outright rapaciousness that had led Elizabeth to build a pirate fleet to humble Spain, or the cold-blooded pragmatism that had served Henry VIII so well as pitted the great powers of Europe against each other.

In 1589 James married Anne, second daughter of Frederick II, king of Denmark. His voyage to meet his bride, whose ship had been driven into a Norwegian port by bad weather, is the only episode of a romantic character in the life of this very prosaic member of a poetic family. By Anne James had three children who survived infancy: Henry Frederick, prince of Wales, who died in 1612; Charles, the future king; and Elizabeth, wife of the elector palatine, Frederick V. He seems to have always been faithful to his wife.

Not the least of James's many ambitions was the desire to excel as an author. He left a body of writings which, though of unremarkable quality as literature, entitle him to a unique place among English kings since Alfred for width of intellectual interest and literary faculty. His first work was in verse, *Essayes of a Prentise in the Divine Art of Poesie* (1584), containing fifteen sonnets, "Ane Metaphoricall invention of a tragedie called Phoenix", a short poem "Of Time", translations from

Du Bartas, Lucan and the Book of Psalms ("out of Tremellius"), and a prose tract entitled "Ane short treatise, containing some Reulis and Cautelis to be observit and eschewit in Scottis Poesie." The volume is introduced by commendatory sonnets, including one by Alexander Montgomerie. The chief interest of the book lies in the "Treatise" and the prefatory sonnets "To the Reader" and "Sonnet decifring the perfyte poete." There is little originality in this youthful production. It has been surmised that it was compiled from the exercises written when the author was Buchanan's pupil at Stirling, and that it was directly suggested by his preceptor's *De Prosodia* and his annotations on *Vives*. On the other hand, it shows intimate acquaintance with the critical reflections of Ronsard and Du Bellay, and of Gascoigne in his *Notes of Instruction* (1575). In 1591 James published *Poeticall Exercises at Vacant Houres*, including a translation of the *Furies* of Du Bartas, his own *Lepanto*, and Du Bartas' version of it, *La Lepanthe*. His *Daemonologie*, a prose treatise in dialog form denouncing witchcraft and exhorting the civil power to the strongest measures of suppression, appeared in 1599. In the same year he printed the first edition (seven copies) of his *Basilikon Doron*, strongly Protestant in tone. A French edition, specially translated for presentation to the pope, has a disingenuous preface explaining that certain phrases (e.g. "papistical doctrine") are omitted, because of the difficulty of rendering them in a foreign tongue. The original edition was, however, translated by order of the suspicious pope, and was immediately placed on the Index. Shortly after going to England James produced his famous *Counterblaste to Tobacco* (1604), in which he forsakes his Scots tongue for Southern English. The volume was published anonymously. James's prose works (including his speeches) were collected and edited (folio, 1616) by James Montagu, bishop of Winchester, and were translated into Latin by the same hand in a companion folio, in 1619. A tract, entitled *The True Law of Free Monarchies*, appeared in 1603; *An Apology for the Oath of Allegiance* in 1607; and a *Declaration du Roy*

BIOGRAPHICAL NOTES

Jacques I. ... pour le droit des Rois in 1615. In 1588 and 1589 James issued two small volumes of *Meditations* on some verses of (a) Revelations and (b) 1 Chronicles. Two other "meditations" were printed posthumously.

Teachers, Sources, and Influences

Young James' regents appointed four tutors to see to his education. The chief of these was George Buchanan, already famous as a poet, humanist, and educator. Buchanan was assisted by Sir Peter Young, the court librarian, and by two noblemen of the Erskine family.[4]

Sir James Melville (1545–1617), a courtier and diplomat who knew James and his teachers, describes their relationship as it existed in the 1570's:

> The twa abbots [Cambuskenneth and Dryburgh] were wyse and modest; my Lady Mar was wyse and schairp, and held [i.e. kept] the King in great aw; and sa did Mester George Buchwhennen. Mester Peter Young was gentiller, and was laith till offend the King at any tym, and used himself wairily, as a man that had mynd of his awin weill, be keeping of his Maiestie's favour. Bot Mester George was a stoik philosopher, and looked not far before the hand; a man of notable qualities for his learning and knawledge in Latin poesie, mekle maid accompt of in other contrees, plaisant in company, re-

---

[4]The Erskines were the abbots of Cambuskenneth and Dryburgh, respectively. However, in an era when clerical appointments were treated essentially as annuities, it is unlikely that either was actually an ordained clergyman.

hersing at all occasions moralities short and fecfull, whereof he had aboundance, and invented wher he wanted.[5]

Buchanan was a strict and impartial schoolmaster who did not shy away from administering punishment, verbal or corporal:

> At one time annoyed by the noise which the King and his playfellows were making, Buchanan bade them be silent under certain penalties if the offence were repeated, and provoked by a childish impertinence from James, took up the little culprit and whipped him with exemplary impartiality, notwithstanding that his companion, the little Master of Mar, stood by, on whom vicarious chastisement might have been applied. Lady Mar, rushing to the scene of action at the sound of "the wailing which ensued", took the child from his master's hands and consoled him in her motherly arms, asking Buchanan indignantly how he dared to touch the Lord's anointed... On another occasion, when the little King tried to get a sparrow from his companion and crushed the bird in the struggle, Buchanan rated him as himself a bird out of a bloody nest.[6]

In 1571, when James was six, Buchanan published a pamphlet titled *Detectio Mariae Reginae* (*Exposure of Queen Mary*) which described Mary as a dangerous monarch, prone to public scandal, and vindicated those who had forced her to abdicate. James, who idolized his mother despite never having known her, came to see Buchanan as an enemy. Nonetheless,

[5]Melville's *Memoirs*, as quoted in Wallace's and Smith's *George Buchanan*.
[6]Oliphant, *Royal Edinburgh: Her Saints, Kings, Prophets, and Poets*

TEACHERS, SOURCES, AND INFLUENCES

Buchanan tried hard to give his pupil the best possible education. Unfortunately, the methods which would have turned a more talented pupil into a great scholar, produced in James "the wisest fool in Christendom"—a walking trove of idealistic theories and Latin quotations who often struggled to apply this knowledge to public policy or even to his personal life.

Buchanan also tried hard to instill a liberal theory of constitutional monarchy in the young king. Even after they parted ways he dedicated three different works to James. In each, he urged him to avoid "the agonisings and wretchedness which await tyrants, even when they seem to be most flourishing outwardly."[7] This too backfired and James became one of the great proponents—at least in theory—of absolute monarchy and the divine right of kings[8]—a theory that would lead the Stuarts to great trouble in the coming years. And yet, even in the *Basilikon Doron*, Buchanan's teachings have a way of creeping back in, as if the absolutist theory was, in fact, an unnatural position for James, which he felt compelled to defend in apology for his mother.

Young James' education, like that of most upper and middle class boys of the 16th century, focused heavily on ancient languages. Buchanan, the foremost Latinist of his generation, would have assigned passages from a variety of classic authors, including Caesar, Cicero, Horace, and Virgil—all of whom are quoted in the *Basilikon Doron*. His Latin reading lists might also have included more modern works. For example, it seems likely that Buchanan would have exposed James to the works of Erasmus, a writer with whom Buchanan had much in common and with whom one of Buchanan's other pupils, Michael de Montaigne, was certainly familiar.

Greek readings would likely have played a secondary role,

---

[7]*De Jure Regni apud Scotos* (1579) as quoted in Wallace's and Smith's *George Buchanan*

[8]His political record told a different story: he rarely opposed Parliament, and never on an issue of importance.

but included Xenophon[9] and Plutarch, both of which James
alludes to frequently in the *Basilikon Doron*. Since Peter
Young's main claim on history (other than tutoring James)
was his possession of one of the finest collections of Greek
works in Europe, James could potentially have had access to
nearly any work in that language. Nevertheless, it is clear
from his writings that he was always better versed in Latin
than Greek.

James' most important source by far was the Bible. Like
most English-speaking Protestants of his era, he knew it mainly
through the *Geneva* translation of 1560[10]—a version notable
for its copious interpretive notes. James also occasionally
quotes directly from the Latin *Vulgate Bible,* which he had
likely studied from in his youth, writing down notable verses
in a personal Latin phrase book.

The *Basilikon Doron* is recognizable as belonging to a type
of philosophical treatise, with which James would have been
quite familiar, in which the author offers advice for an ideal
ruler. These "Mirrors for Princes" make up a literary tradi-
tion going back at least as far as James' beloved *Cyropaedia,*
by Xenophon. While the *Doron* is unusual in that the author was an actual ruler, it is otherwise representative of the
type. This ancient genre enjoyed a revival of popularity in the
late Renaissance, with authors as diverse as Erasmus[11] and
Machiavelli[12] trying their hands at it (as well as many lesser
lights). Since real princes tend to already know the informa-
tion in these books, and either apply it or reject it in the

---

[9]Readings from Xenophon, then as now, were often assigned to beginning Greek students because he used a very simple and direct form of
Attic Greek.

[10]The Geneva Bible was revised in 1599 and much of its text was later
incorporated in the Authorized ("King James") version.

[11]Erasmus' *The Education of a Christian Price* (1516) was addressed to
Charles V.

[12]It has been argued that Machiavelli's *Prince* is not so much an example
of the genre as a satire of it, yet there can be little doubt that it is a
sincere representation of Machiavelli's political philosophy.

face of political reality, the real purpose is to provide a framework for the presentation of the philosopher's political and historical theories. While James clearly intended that his sons (especially Henry, the heir-apparent) read the *Doron*, the real purpose would have been to codify the knowledge of king-craft of which he was so proud.

In his addendum "To the Reader" James claims that the *Doron* was never intended for public consumption and that he only published the second edition after one or more of the original copies had been leaked to the public. It has often been pointed out that the candid views expressed therein had the effect of alienating certain groups (Puritans, Roman Catholics, Gaelic Scots, etc.), providing further proof of unintentional distribution. In fact, however, James never had much chance of winning these people to his camp; hence he had little to loose in that regard. Actually, the most successful policies of his reign were focused on limiting the influence of ("oppressing") these very groups. This was even more the case after inheriting England, when James realized the desirability of improving relations with the Church of England. In this light, the *Doron* can be understood as a piece of political propaganda to impress those whose support James needed at the risk of angering those who already distrusted and opposed him. Thus the timing of the release of the second edition in 1603, the same year James traveled to London to take the English throne, seems rather convenient.

Political implications aside, however, the *Doron* is typical of James' works in that it demonstrates an overwhelming desire to establish legitimacy: both as a scholar and as a king. Throughout his writing we are conscious of a nagging impression of the king's fundamental insecurity, forcing him to continually justify himself. James was aware, on some level, that he was only a middling scholar, and suspected that he wasn't worthy of the kingship. Was this awareness of his inferiority the very defect in his character that kept him mired in mediocrity throughout his career?

King James' English

English at the turn of the seventeenth century was far from standardized; vocabulary and syntax were still heavily regional, while spelling and punctuation were largely a matter of an author's whim, and could change multiple times in the same work—or even in the same sentence. This apparent chaos reflects English's youth as a literary language (beginning only with Chaucer in the previous century) as well as the high level of social change in the Elizabethan and Jacobean periods.

Ironically, James indirectly did more than anyone else to eventually standardize the language via his sponsorship of the authorized translation of the Bible and his patronage of William Shakespeare. The "King James" Bible and Shakespeare's plays would become the cornerstones of English literature for the next three centuries, affecting the language of nearly every writer after James' time.

James' own style, however, belonged to an earlier age, and contained plenty of idiosyncrasies all his own. To begin with, he was raised in Scotland. Early drafts of the *Doron* were probably written completely in the Scots language.[13] By the time of publication James had revised his manuscript closer to "English," but the version we have is still studded liberally with Scots words and idioms.

Next, like all educated people of his time, he had been trained from a young age to read and write Latin, a language

---

[13] A language that is roughly as different from English as Portuguese is from Spanish. Not to be confused with Scots Gaelic.

with quite a different sentence structure than English. The ideal Latin sentence (according to Cicero and other Golden Age Latinists) is a paragraph length construct known as a "period". A typical Latin period introduces the subject and object nouns then follows with multiple sub-clauses before finally ending with a verb. To James and other Early Modern writers good style consisted of as close an imitation as possible of the Latin period, regardless of the language used. This produced long and convoluted sentences, as judged by the standards of twenty-first century English.

Finally, James seems to have had a difficult time balancing his desire to use an informal tone, appropriate to a father addressing his son, with his need to demonstrate his learning and erudition. The result is prose that oscillates between the chatty and the pedantic.

Once allowances are made for these factors, however, the *Basilikon Doron* is a surprisingly effective work for a man for whom writing was basically a hobby. It provides a fascinating look into the mind of a historically important, yet often misunderstood, ruler.

Notes on this Edition

Words that are still in common usage are silently corrected to reflect contemporary American spelling. Articles are replaced with their modern equivalents (e.g. "ye" is changed to "you"). Words are inflected according to modern usage, except in verse passages when doing so would damage the meter. Punctuation is modernized as long as doing so preserves the basic sentence structure. Archaic and Scots words are defined in the footnotes below the first usage and again in the glossary at the rear of the book.

I have endeavored to provide translations of all of James' Latin, Greek, and French quotations. I must apologize in advance for any errors, particularly in translations from Ancient Greek—a language of which I have little knowledge and for which I was forced to rely heavily on machine translation.

Whenever possible I have noted references and quotations from other works but, unfotunately, there were a few which I was not able to track down. James sometimes alludes to some fairly obscure (in this century, at least) books, and frequently makes his own—liberal—translations of passages from memory.

Basilikon Doron

Dedication

Lo hear (my son) a mirror vive.[14] and fair
Which showeth the shadow of a worthy king.
Lo here a book, a pattern doth you bring
Which you should preasse[15] to follow
          more and more.
This trusty friend, the truth will never spare,   5
But give a good advice unto you here:
How it should be your chief and princely care,
To follow virtue, vice for to forbear.
And in this book your lesson will you learn,
For guiding of your people great and small.   10
Then (as you ought) give an attentive ear,
And panse[16] how you these precepts practice shall.
    You father bids you study here and reede.[17]
    How to become a perfite[18] king indeed.

---

[14]**vive** alive; vivid; lively
[15]**preasse** to attempt
[16]**panse** consider or meditate on
[17]**reede** to take counsel or become aware
[18]**perfite** perfect, skillful, or complete

Argument of the Book

God gives not kings the style of gods in vain,
For on his throne his scepter do they sway:
And as their subjects ought them to obey,
So kings should fear and serve their God again.
If then you would enjoy a happy reign,   5
Observe the statutes of your heavenly king;
And from his law make all your laws to spring:
Since his lieutenant here you should remain.
Reward the just, be steadfast, true, and plain:
Repress the proud, maintaining aye[19] the right,   10
Walk always so, as ever in his sight
Who guards the godly, plaguing the profane,
    And so you shall in princely virtues shine.
    Resembling right your mighty king divine.

---

[19] **aye** always; still

Epistle

To Henry[20] my dearest son and natural successor,

Whomto can so rightly appertain this book of the institution of a prince in all the points of his calling, as well general (as a Christian towards God) as particular (as a king towards his people)? Whomto (I say) can it so justly appertain, as unto you my dearest son? Since I the author thereof as your natural father, must be careful for your godly and virtuous education as my eldest son and the first fruits of God's blessing towards me in my posterity, and (as a king) must timously[21] provide for your training up in all points of a king's office (since you are my natural and lawful successor therein) that (being rightly informed hereby of the weight of your burden) you may in time begin to consider that, being born to be a king, you are rather born to *onus*, than *honos*,[22] not excelling all your people so far in rank and honor as in daily care and hazardous painstaking, for the dutiful administration of that great office that God hath laid upon your shoulders—laying so a just symmetry and proportion betwixt the height of your honorable place and the heavy weight of your great charge and consequently, in case of failure (which God forbid), of the sadness of your fall, according to the proportion of that height. I have there-

---

[20]Henry, Prince of Wales (d. 1616)
[21]**timously** in good time
[22]**onos,** *than* **honos** *burden,* than *honor*

[7]

fore (for the greater ease to your memory and that you may, at the first, cast up any part that you have to do with) divided this whole book in three parts. The first teaches you your duty towards God as a Christian, the next your duty in your office as a king, and the third teaches you how to behave yourself in indifferent things which of themselves are neither right nor wrong, but according as they are rightly or wrong used, and yet will serve (according to your behavior therein) to augment or impair your fame and authority at the hands of your people. Receive and welcome this book, then, as a faithful preceptor and counselor unto you which (because my affairs will not permit me ever to be present with you) I ordain to be a resident faithful admonisher of you. And because the hour of death is uncertain to me (as unto all flesh) I leave it as my testament and latter will unto you: charging you in the presence of God, and by the fatherly authority I have over you that you keep it ever with you, as carefully as Alexander did the *Iliad* of Homer.[23]

You will find it a just and impartial counselor, neither flattering you in any vice, nor importuning you at unmeete times: It will not come uncalled, not speak unspeered at:[24] and yet conferring with it when you are quiet, you shall say with Scipio, that you're *nunquam minus solus, quam cum solus.*[25]

To conclude then, I charge you (as ever you think to deserve my fatherly blessing) to follow and put in practice (as far as lies in you) the precepts following. And if you follow the contrary course, I take the great God to record that this book shall one

---

[23]From Plutarch's *Parallel Lives* in which he states that Alexander "...was naturally a great lover of all kinds of learning and reading...he constantly laid Homer's Iliads...with his dagger under his pillow, declaring that he esteemed it a perfect portable treasure of all military virtue and knowledge."

[24]**unspeered at** unspoken to

[25]**nunquam...solus** *never less lonely than when alone.* Part of a quotation of Scipio Africanus (236–184/3 BCE) preserved by Cato the Elder, as quoted in Cicero's *De Officiis*, III:1. The full quote is "never less at leisure than when at leisure, nor less lonely than when alone"

day be a witness betwixt me and you, and shall procure to be ratified in heaven, the curse that in that case here I give you; for I protest before that great God, I had rather be not a father and childless, nor be a father of wicked children. But (hoping, yea even promising unto myself, that God who in his great blessing sent you unto me, shall in the same blessing as he hath given me a Son, so make him a good and godly son, not repenting him of his mercy shown unto me) I end this preface with my earnest prayer to God to work effectually into you the fruits of that blessing which here from my heart, I bestow upon you.

Finis.

Book I: Anent a King's Christian Duty Towards God

As he can not be thought worthy to rule and command others that cannot rule and dantone[26] his own proper affections and unreasonable appetites, so can he not be thought worthy to govern a Christian people, knowing and fearing God, that in his own person and heart fears not, and loves not the divine majesty. Neither can anything in his government succeed well with him (devise and labor as he list), as coming from a filthy spring, if his person be unsanctified, for (as David says), "In vain watcheth thou the Citie, or buyldest thou the house, if the Lord by his blessing grant not successe therunto"[27] and as Paul says, "Cephas may plant, and Apollo may water, but it is God only that may give the increase."[28] Therefore (my son), first of all things, learn to know and love that God whomto you have a double obligation: first, for that he made you a man, and next, for that he made you a little god to sit on his throne and rule over other men. Remember that as in dignity he hath erected you above others, so ought you in

---

[25]**anent** regarding, about

[26]**dantone** subdue or tame

[27]Ps 127:1 "Except the Lord buylde the house, thei labour in vaine that buylde it: except the Lord kepe the citie, the keeper watcheth in vaine."

[28]1 Cor 3:6 "I have planted, Apollos watred, but God gave the encrease."

thankfulness towards him go as far beyond all others. A mote in another's eye is a beam into yours;[29] a blemish in another, is a leprous boil into you, and a venial sin (as the Papists call it) in another is a great crime into you. Think not therefore that the highness of your dignity diminishes your faults (much less gives you a license to sin) but, by the contrary, your fault shall be aggravated according to the height of your dignity—any sin that you commit not being a single sin procuring but the fall of one but being an exemplar sin, and therefore draws with it the whole multitude to be guilty of the same. Remember then, that this glistering[30] worldly glory of kings is given them by God to teach them to preasse so to glister and shine before their people in all works of sanctification and righteousness that their persons as bright lamps of godliness and virtue may (going in and out before their people) give light to all their steps. Remember also, that by the right knowledge, and fear of God (which is the beginning of wisdom, as Solomon says)[31] you shall know all the things necessary for the discharge of your duty, both as a Christian and as a king, seeing in him (as in a mirror) the course of all earthly things, whereof he is the spring and only mover.

Now the only way to bring you to this knowledge is diligently to read his word and earnestly to pray for the right understanding thereof. Search the scriptures (says Christ)[32] for they will bear testimony of me; and the whole scriptures (says Paul)[33] are profitable to teach, to improve, to correct, and to instruct in righteousness that the man of God may be

---

[29] An allusion to Lk 6:41–42

[30] **glistering** glittering, shining

[31] Prov 9:10 "The beginning of wisdome is the fear of the Lord, & the knowledge of holy things is understanding."

[32] Jn 5:39 "Searche the Scriptures: for in them ye thinke to have eternal life, & thei are thei which testifie of me." Note, though, that this is taken out of context from a passage that stresses that faith in Christ is even more important than knowledge of the scriptures.

[33] 2 Tim 3:16–17 "For the whole Scripture is given by inspiration of God, and is profitable to teache, to improve, to correct, and to instructe in

absolute, being made perfite unto all good works. I join to this the careful hearing of the doctrine with attendance and reverence, for faith comes by hearing (says Paul).[34] But above all, beware you thraw[35] not the word to your appetite, (as over-many do) making it like a bell to sound as you please to interpret. But by the contrary, frame all your affections to follow precisely the rules there set down.

The whole scripture contains but two things: a command, and a prohibition; to do such things, and abstain from the contrary. Obey in both; neither think it enough to abstain from evil and do no good, nor think not that if you do many good things it may serve you for a cloak to mix evil turns therewith. And as in these two points the whole scripture consists, so in two degrees stands the whole service of God by man: interior, or upward; exterior, or downward—the first, by prayer in faith towards God; the next, by works flowing therefore before the world, which is nothing else but the exercise of religion towards God, and of equity towards your neighbor.

As for the particular points of religion, I need not to delate[36] them; I am no hypocrite, follow your father's footsteps and your own education therein. I thank God, I was never ashamed to give account of my profession, howsoever the malicious lying tongues of some have traduced me. And if my conscience had not resolved me that all my religion was grounded upon the plain words of scripture I had never outwardly avowed it for pleasure or awe of the vain pride of some seditious preachers.

And as for the points of equity towards your neighbor (because that will fall in properly upon the second part concerning a king's office) I leave it to the own room.

---

righteousnes, that the man of God may be absolute, being made perfite unto all good workes."

[34]Rom 10:17 "Then faith is by hearing, & hearing by the worde of God."

[35]**thraw** twist, wrench, wreathe, cast, or throw

[36]**delate** explain or discourse at length

For the first part then, of man's service to his God (which is religion), that is, the worship of God according to his revealed will, it is wholly grounded upon the scripture (as I have already said) quickened by faith, and conserved by conscience. For the scripture, I have already spoken of it in general but that you may the more readily make choice of any part thereof for your instruction or comfort remember only this method.

The whole scripture is dited[37] by Gods spirit, thereby (as by his lively word) to instruct and rule the whole Church Militant, till the end of the world. It is composed of two parts, the Old and New Testament. The ground of the former is the law, which shares our sin and contains justice. The ground of the other is Christ who, pardoning sin, contains grace. The sum of the law is the Ten Commands, more largely delated in the law, interpreted by the prophets. And by histories are the examples shown of obedience or disobedience thereto, and what *praemium* or *poena*[38] was accordingly given by God. But because no man was able to keep the law, nor any part thereof, it pleased God of his infinite wisdom and goodness to incarnate his only son in our nature for satisfaction of his justice in his suffering for us, that since we could not be saved by doing, we might (at least) be saved by believing. The ground therefore of the law of grace, is contained in the four histories of the birth, life, death, and resurrection of Christ.[39]

The larger interpretation of this law is contained in the epistles of the apostles, and the practice in the faithful or unfaithful, together with their reward or punishment according thereto, is contained in the *Acts of the Apostles.*

Would you then know your sin by the saw? Read the books of Moses containing it. Would you have a commentary thereupon? Read the prophets Would you see how good men are rewarded and wicked punished? Look the histories of Genesis,

---

[37]**dited** dictated, written
[38]**praemium** *or* **poena** *recompense* or *fine*
[39]i.e. the four gospels

Exodus, Joshua, the Judges, Job, and Ester, but especially the books of the Kings, and Chronicles, wherewith you ought to be familiarly acquainted: for there will you see yourself (as in a mirror) either among the catalogs of the good or evil kings.

Would you know the life and death of Christ? Look the evangelists. Would you be more particularly trained up in his school? Meditate upon the epistles of the apostles. And would you be acquainted with the practices of that doctrine in the persons of the primitive church? Cast up the apostles' Acts. As to the apocryphal books, I omit them because I am no Papist (as I said before) and indeed some of them are as like the ditement[40] of the spirit of God, as an egg is to an oyster.

But when you read the scripture, read it with a sanctified and chaste ear. Admire reverently such obscure places as you understand not, blaming only your own incapacity. Read with delight the plain places and study carefully to understand those that are somewhat difficile:[41] preasse to be a good textuary,[42] for the scripture is ever the best interpreter of itself. But preasse not curiously to seek out farther nor is contained therein, for that were misnurtured[43] presumption, to strive to be farther upon God's secrets nor he hath will you be, for what he thought needful for us to know, that hath he revealed there. And delight most in reading such parts of scripture as may best serve your instruction in your calling, rejecting foolish curiosities upon numbers and genealogies, which are but vain and profit not (as Paul says).[44]

Now, as to faith, which is the entertainer and quickener of religion (as I have else said), it is a sure persuasion and apprehension of the promises of God, applying them to your soul, and therefore may it justly be called the golden chain

---

[40]**ditement** something indited or dictated by another

[41]**difficile** difficult

[42]**textuary** one who is knowledgeable about sacred texts

[43]**misnurtured** ill bred

[44]Titus 3:9 "But stay foolish questions, and genealogies, and contentions, and brawlings about the Law: for thei are unprofitable & vaine."

that links the faithful soul to Christ. And, because it grows not in our garden but is the free gift of God (as Paul says),[45] it must be nourished by prayer, which is nothing else but a friendly talking with God. Use oft to pray when you are quietest, especially in your bed, for public prayer serves more for example (for the most part) than for any particular comfort to the supplicant. In your prayer, be neither over-strange with God (like the ignorant common sort that pays nothing but out of books) nor yet over-homely[46] with him (like some of our vain proud Puritans, that think they rule him upon their fingers). The former way will breed an uncouth coldness in you towards him. The other will breed in you a contempt of him. But, in your prayer to God, speak with all reverence, for if a subject will not speak but reverently to a king, much less should any flesh presume to crak[47] with God as his companion.

Crave in your prayer not only things spiritual but corporeal, whiles things of greater, and whiles of less consequence, that you may lay up in store his grant of these things for confirmation of your faith, and to be an arles-pennie[48] unto you of his love. Pray as you find your heart moves you *pro re nata*[49] but see that you suit no unlawful things—as revenge, lust, or such like—for that prayer can not come of faith, and prayer without faith is sin (as Paul says).[50] When you obtain your prayer, thank him joyfully therefore. If otherwise, bear patiently, preassing to win him with importunity as the widow did Christ.[51] And if, notwithstanding, thereof you be

---

[45]Phil 1:29 "For unto you it is given for Christ, that not onely ye shulde beleve in him, but also suffer for his sake,"

[46]**over-homely** overly familiar

[47]**crak** talk, converse

[48]**arles-pennie** earnest money; a pledge to seal a bargain

[49]**pro re nata** *for the present matter* i.e. as needed

[50]Rom 14:23 "For he that douteth, is condemned if he eat, because he eateth not of faith: & whatsoever is not of faith, is sinne." Note, however, that the passage from which this is taken applies more to the applicability of the Mosaic food laws to gentiles than to prayer.

[51]Mt 15:22–23 "And beholde, a woman, a Cananite came out of the same

not heard, assure yourself God foresees that which you ask is not for your weill;[52] and learn in time so to interpret all the adversities that God shall send unto you, so shall you in the midst of them not only be armed with patience, but joyfully lift up your eyes from the present trouble, to the happy end that God will turn it to. And when you find it once so fall out by proof, arm yourself with the experience thereof against the next trouble, assuring yourself (although you cannot in time of the shower see through the clouds yet) in the end, you will find God sent it for your weill, as you found in the former.

And as for conscience (which I called the conserver of religion), it is nothing else but the light of knowledge that God has planted in man which choppes[53] him with a feeling that he has done wrong whenever he commits any sin. And surely, although this conscience be a great torture to the wicked, yet is as great a comfort to the godly, if we will consider it rightly. For have we not a great advantage that have within ourselves while we live here a counte book[54] and inventory of all the crimes that we will be accused of, either at the hour of our death, or at the great day of judgment, which when we please (yea if we forget) it will choppe, and remember us to look upon, that while we have leisure and are here, we may remember to amend, and so at the day of our trial, compeere[55] with new and white garments washed in the blood of the Lamb (as Saint John says).[56] Above all then (my son), labor to keep sound

---

coasts, and cryed, saying unto him, Have mercie on me, o Lord, the sonne of David: my daughter is miserably vexed with a devil. But he answered her not a worde. Then came to him his disciples, and besoght him, saying, Send her away, for she cryeth after us."

[52] **weill** benefit, advantage

[53] **choppes** strikes, attacks rudely, or flogs

[54] **counte book** account book

[55] **compeere** present one's self in court after being summoned

[56] Rev 7:14 "And I said unto him, Lord, thou knowest. And he said to me, These are they, which came out of great tribulacion, and have washed their long robes & have made their long robes white in the blood of the Lambe."

this conscience which many prattle of, but over-few feel. Especially be careful to keep it free from two diseases, which it uses oft to be infected with, to wit: leprosy, and superstition. The former is the mother of atheism, the other of heresies. By a leprous conscience I mean a cauterized conscience (as Paul calls it)[57] being become senseless of sin, through sleeping in a careless security, as King David's was after his murder and adultery, aye while he was wakened by prophet Nathan's similitude.[58] And for superstition, the word itself is plain enough, being *vocabulum artis*.[59]

As for a preservative against this leprosy, remember ever once in the four and twenty hours, either in the night, or when you are at greatest quiet, to call yourself to account of all your last day's actions, either wherein you have committed things you should not, or omitted the things you should do, either in your Christian or kingly calling and in that account, let not yourself be smoothed over with that flattering $\phi\iota\lambda\alpha\nu\tau\iota\alpha$,[60] (which is over kindly a sickness to all mankind) but censure yourself as sharply as if you were your own enemy, for if you judge yourself, you shall not be judged (as Paul says)[61] and syne,[62] according to your censure, reform your actions as far as you may, eschewing ever willfully and willingly to contrary your conscience, for a small sin willfully committed, with a deliberate resolution to break the bridle of conscience therein, is far grievouser before God than a greater sin committed in a sudden passion when conscience is asleep. Remember therefore in all your actions of the great account that you are one day

---

[57] 1 Tim 4:2 "...[w]hich speake lyes through hypocrise, and have their consciences burned with an hote yron,"
[58] 2 Sam 12:1–15
[59] **vocabulum artis** *a narrow term*
[60] $\phi\iota\lambda\alpha\nu\tau\iota\alpha$ *egoism or self love*
[61] 1 Cor 11:31 "For if we wolde judge our selves, we shulde not be judged"
[62] **syne** afterwords, later

to make, in all the days of your life ever learning to die, and living every day as it were your last:

Omnem crede diem tibi diluxisse supremum.[63]

And therefore I would not have you to pray with the Papists, to be preserved from sudden death, but that God would give you grace so to live as you may every hour of your life be ready for death; so shall you attain to the virtue of true fortitude, never being afraid for the horror of death, come when he list. And especially, beware to offend your conscience with use of swearing or lying (suppose but in mowes)[64] for oaths are but a use, and a sin clothed with no delight nor gain, and therefore inexcusable before God. And lying comes also much of a vile use by banishing shame: therefore beware even to deny the truth, which is a sort of lie that may best be eschewed by a person of your rank, for if anything be speered at you that you think not meet to reveal, if you say that question is not pertinent for them to speer, who dare examine you further? And using this answer whiles both in true and false things that will be speered at you, these misnurtured people will never be the wiser thereof.

And for keeping your conscience sound from that sickness of superstition, which is called *morbus animi*,[65] you must neither lay the safety of your conscience upon the credit of your own conceits, nor yet of other men's humors, how great doctors of divinity that ever they be; but you must only ground it upon the express scripture, for conscience not grounded upon sure knowledge, is either an ignorant fantasy, or an arrogant glaikerie.[66]

Beware therefore in this case with two extremities: the one to believe (with the Papists) the church's authority, better

[63]**Omnem...supremum** *Believe every day is your last.* Horace, *Epistles* I:4:13
[64]**mowes** mocks or jests
[65]**morbus animi** *disease of the soul*
[66]**glaikerie** folly, caprice

nor your own knowledge, the other to lean (with the Anabaptists)[67] to your own conceits and dreamed revelations.

But learn wisely to discern betwixt points of substance and ceremonies, and betwixt the express commandment and will of God in his word and the invention or ordinance of man, since all that is necessary for salvation is contained in the scripture. For in anything that is expressly commanded or prohibited in the book of God you cannot be over-precise even in the least thing, counting every sin (not according to the light estimation and common use of it in the world) but as the book of God counts it. But as for all other things not contained in the scripture, spare not to use or alter them as the necessity of the time shall require. And when any of the spiritual office bearers in the church speak unto you anything that is well warranted by the word reverence and obey them as the heralds of the most high God but (if passing that bounds) they would urge you to embrace any of their fantasies in place of God's word, or would color their particulars with a pretended zeal, acknowledge them for vain people passing the bounds of their calling and (according to your office) gravely and with authority redact them in odor again.

To conclude then, both this purpose of conscience and the first part of this book, keep God sparingly in your mouth, but abundantly in your heart. Be precise in effect but social in show. Kithe[68] more by your deeds nor by your words the love of virtue and hatred of vice: and delight more to be godly and virtuous in deed, nor to be thought and called so, expecting more for your prize and reward in heaven nor here; and apply to all your outward actions Christ's command, to give alms secretly: so shall you on the one part be inwardly garnished with true Christian humility, not outwardly (with the proud

---

[67]**Anabaptists** a radical protestant sect that first arose in the 16th century. They believed in adult baptism and a strict interpretation of the Bible, including avoiding oaths and military service. The sect eventually evolved into the modern Mennonite and Amish churches.
[68]**kithe** to show, make known by one's actions

Pharisee) glorying in your godliness but saying (as Christ commands us all) when we have done all that we can, *Inutiles servi sumus*;[69] and on the other part, you shall eschew outwardly before the world, the suspicion of filthy proud hypocrisy and deceitful dissimulation.

---

[69]**Inutiles servi sumus** *We are unprofitable servants.* Lk 17:10 "So likewise ye, when ye have done all those things, which are commanded you, say, We are unprofitable servants: we have done that which was our dutie to do."

Book II: Anent a King's Duty in His Office

But as you are clothed with two callings, so must you be alike careful for the discharge of them both: that as you are a good Christian, so you may be a good king, discharging your office (as I showed before) in the points of justice and equity: which in two sundry ways you must do: the one, in establishing and executing (which is the life of the law) good laws among your people, the other, by your behavior in your own person and with your servants, to teach your people by your example; for people are naturally inclined to counterfeit (like apes) their prince's manners, according to that old verse

Regis ad exemplum[70]

For the part of making and executing laws, consider first the true difference betwixt a lawful good King, and a usurping tyrant and you shall the more easily understand your duty herein, for *contraria contrariis opposita magis illucescunt.*[71] The one acknowledge himself ordained for his people, having received from God a burden of government whereof he must be countable: The other thinks his people ordained for him, a prey to his appetites, as the fruits of his magnanimity; and

---

[70]**Regis ad exemplum** *To the example of the king.* Claudian, *Panegyricus de Quarto Consulatu Honorii Augusti* Line 300
[71]**contraria...illucescunt** *contraries illustrate better when placed opposite their contraries.* Cicero, *Topica.* Chapter XI

therefore, as their ends are directly contrary, so are their whole actions (as middeses)[72] whereby they press to attain their ends. A good King (thinking his highest honor to consist in the due discharge of his calling) employs all his study and pains to procure and maintain (by the making and execution of good laws) the welfare and peace of his people and (as their natural father and kindly master) thinks his greatest contentment stands in their prosperity and his greatest surety in having their hearts, subjecting his own private affections and appetites to the weill and standing of his subjects, ever thinking the common interest his chieftest particular: where, by the contrary, a usurping tyrant (thinking his greatest honor and felicity to consist in attaining, *per fas, vel nefas,*[73] to his ambitious pretenses) thinking never himself sure, but by the dissension and factions among his people, and counterfeiting the saint while he once creep in credit, will then (by inverting all good laws to serve only for his unruly private affections) frame the commonweal ever to advance his particular: building his surety upon his peoples misery: and in end (as a stepfather and an uncouth hireling) make up his own hand upon the ruins of the republic. And according to their actions, so receive they their reward: For a good king (after a happy and famous reign) dies in peace, lamented by his subjects, and admired by his neighbors: and leaving a reverent renown behind him on earth, obtains the crown of eternal felicity in heaven: And although some of them (which falls out very rarely) may be cut off by the treason of some unnatural subjects, yet lives their fame after them, and some notable plague misses never to overtake the committers, who will be infamous to all posterity: Where

---

[72]**middeses** means

[73]**per fas, vel nefas** *through right and wrong* "[U]nfair eristic treatment. It occurs when interlocutor A postulates a theory, and cites several reasons that justify it. Interlocutor B then refutes one of the arguments, and triumphantly declares that A's argument has no basis, even though he never said a word about the other arguments that A put forth." *Wikipedia*

by the contrary, a tyrant's miserable and infamous life, arms in end his own subjects to become his burreaux:[74] And although that rebellion be ever unlawful on their part, yet is the world so wearied of him, that his fall is little meaned[75] by the rest of his subjects, and but smiled at by his neighbors: And besides the infamous memory he leaves behind him here, and he endless pains he sustains hereafter, it oft falls out, that the committers not only escape unpunished, but farther, the fact will remain as allowed by the law in divers ages thereafter. It is easy then for you (my son) to make a choice of one of these two sorts of rulers, by following the way of virtue to establish your standing, yes, in case you fall in the highway, yet should it be with the honorable report and just regret of all honest men.

And therefore to return to my purpose anent the government of your subjects, by making and putting good laws to execution, I remit the making of them to your own discretion, as you shall find the necessity of new-rising corruptions to require them: for *Ex malis moribus bonae leges:*[76] besides, that in the country we have already more good laws than are well executed, and am only to insist in your form of government anent their execution: only remember, that as parliaments are only ordained for making of laws, so abuse not their constitution, in holding them for any men's particulars. For as a parliament is the honorablest and highest judgment in the land (as being the king's head court) if it be well used, which is by the making of good laws in it; so is it the injustest judgment seat that may be, being abused to men's particulars: irrevocable decrees against particular parties being given therein under color of general laws, and ofttimes the estates not knowing themselves whom thereby they hurt: And therefore hold no parliaments but for necessity of new laws, which

---

[74]**burreaux** hangmen
[75]**meaned** lamented
[76]**Ex...leges** *From bad customs come good laws.* proverbial

would be but seldom; for few laws and well put in execution, are best in a well ruled commonweal. As for the matter of fore-faltures[77] (which also are done in Parliament) it is not good tigging[78] with these things; but my advice is, you forefalt none but for such odious crimes as may make them unworthy ever to be restored again: and for smaller offenses, you have other penalties sharp enough to be used against them.

And as for the execution of good laws (whereat I left) remember that among the differences that I put betwixt the forms of the government of a good king, and an usurping tyrant: I shew how a tyrant would enter like a saint while he found himself fast underfoot, and then would suffer his unruly affections to burst forth: Therefore be you contrary at your first entry to your kingdom, to yon *Quinquennium Neronis,*[79] with his tender-hearted wish, *"Utinam nescirem literas"*[80] in giving the law full execution against all breakers thereof but exception; for since you come not to your reign *precario,*[81] nor by conquest, but by right and due descent; fear no uproars for doing of justice, since you may assure yourself, the most part of your people will ever naturally favor justice, providing always, that you do it only for love to justice, and not for satisfying any particular passions of yours under color thereof: otherwise, how justly that ever the offender deserve it, you are guilty of murder before God: for you must consider, that God ever looks to your inward intention in all your actions. And when you have by the severity of justice once settled your countries, and made them know that you can strike, then

---

[77]**forefaltures** judiciary forfeitures of property

[78]**tigging** touching lightly, dallying with

[79]**Quinquennium Neronis** The first five happy years of the Emperor Nero's reign before his administration descended into autocracy and misrule. Literally *Nero's five-year period*

[80]**Utinam nescirem literas,** *Would that I was ignorant of letters!* Nero's purported exclamation upon an occasion of signing a man's death warrant. Suetonius, *The Lives of the Twelve Caesars* 6:10

[81]**precario** *serendipitously; doubtfully*

may you thereafter all the days of your life mix justice with mercy, punishing or sparing, as you shall find the crime to have been willfully or rashly committed, and according to the bypast behavior of the committer: for if otherwise you kithe your clemency at the first, the offenses would soon come to such heaps, and the contempt of you grow so great, that when you would fall to punish, the number of them to be punished would exceed the punishers, and you would be troubled to resolve whomat to begin, and (against your nature) would be compelled then to wrack many, which the chastisement of few in the beginning might have preserved: but in this, my overdear cost experience may serve you for a sufficient lesson, for I confess, where I thought (by being gracious at the beginning) to win all men's hearts to a loving and willing obedience, I by the contrary found, the disorder of the country and the tinsell[82] of my thanks to be all my reward.

But as this severe justice of yours upon all offenses would be but for a time (as I have already said) so are there some horrible crimes that you are bound in conscience never to forgive: such as witchcraft, willful murder, incest (especially within the degrees of consanguinity) sodomy, poisoning, and false coin: as for treason against your own person or authority, (since the fault concerns yourself) I remit to your own choice to punish or pardon therein as your heart serves you, and according to the circumstances of the turn and the quality of the committer.

Here would I also eike[83] another crime to be unpardonable, if I would not be thought partial: but the fatherly love I bear you, will make me break the bounds of shame in opening it unto you. It is this, the unreverent writing or speaking of your parents and predecessors: you know the command in God's law, "Honor your father and mother":[84] and consequently (since you are the lawful magistrate) suffer not both

---

[82]**tinsell** loss

[83]**eike** add, augment, or increase

[84]Ex 20:12 "Honor they father and thy mother, that thy dais maie be prolonged upon the land which the Lord thy God giveth thee."

your princes and your parents to be dishonored by any: I grant
we have all our faults, which (privately betwixt you and God)
should serve you for examples to meditate upon and mend in
your person, but (should not be a matter of discourse to others; since you are come of as honorable predecessors as any
prince living, *Sepeliatur synagoga cum honor:*[85] and I prey
you, how can they love you that hate them whom of you are
come? Wherefore destroy men innocent young sucking wolves
and foxes? But for the hatred they bear to their race: and
why will a colt of a courser of Naples finds a greater price in
a market than an ass colt but for the love of the father: it is
therefore a thing monstrous, to see a man love the child and
hate the parents. And for conclusion of this point, I may also
allege my own experience, for besides the judgments of God
that with my eyes I have seen fall upon all them that were
chief traitors to my parents, I may justly affirm, I never found
yet a constant biding by me in all my straits, by any that were
of perfite age in my parents' days, but only by such as constantly bode by them, I mean specially, by them that served
the queen my mother: for so that I discharge my conscience to
you (my son) in revealing you the truth, I care not what any
traitor or treason allower think of it.

And although the crime of oppression be not in this rank
of unpardonable crimes, yet the over-common use of it in this
nation, as it is were a virtue (especially by the greatest rank of
subjects in the land) requires the king to be a sharp censurer
thereof. Be diligent therefore to try, and awful to beat down
the hornes[86] of proud officers: Embrace the quarrel of the poor

---

[85]**Sepeliatur...honor** *The synagogue may with honor be suppressed.* The
term "synagogue" in this period referred not only to Jewish congre-
gations but often also to illegitimate Christian sects. James is speaking mainly about Scottish protestants who were critical of his mother,
Mary, because she had been Catholic and had frequently been in open
conflict with John Knox and other radical Protestants.
[86]**hornes** legal procedures in which a defendant was denounced as a
rebel or traitor in the Scots courts

and distressed as your own particular, thinking it your greatest honor to repress the oppressors: Care for the pleasure of none, nor spare no pains in your person to see their wrongs redressed: And remember of the honorable stile given to my grandfather, in being called "the poor man's king", and as the most part of a king's office, stands in deciding that question of *meum* and *tuum*,[87] among his subjects. Remember when you sit in judgment, that the throne you sit on is God's (as Kind David says) and sway neither to the right hand nor to the left: either loving the rich or pitying the poor: justice should be blind and friendless: It is not there you should reward your friends nor cross your enemies.

Here now speaking of oppressors and of justice, the purpose leads me to speak of Highland and Border oppressions. As for the Highlands, I shortly comprehend them all in two sorts of people: the one, that dwells in our mainland that are barbarous, and yet mixed with some show of civility: the other, that dwell in the isles and are utterly barbarous, without any sort of show of civility. For the first sort, put straitly to execution the laws made already by me against their overlords and the chiefs of their clans, and it will be no difficulty to dantone them. As for the other sort, think no other of them all, than as of wolves and wild boars, And therefore follow forth the course that I have begun, in planting colonies among them of answerable inland subjects,[88] that within short time may root them out and plant civility in their rooms. But as for the Borders because I know, if you enjoy not this whole isle according to God's right and your lineal descent, you will never get leave to brook this North and barrenest part thereof, no, not your own head whereon the crown should stand: I need not in that

---

[87]**meum** and **tuum** *mine and yours* q.v. Hobbes, *Leviathan*,18:7,8

[88]James' strategy of settling lowland Scots in problem areas was successful enough that he went on (as King of England) to apply it in North Ireland, a decision which has had considerable historical repercussions.

case trouble you with them, for then they will be the midst of the isle, and so as easily ruled as any part thereof.

And that you may the readier wisdom and justice govern your subjects, by knowing what vices they are naturally most inclined to, as a good physician, who must first know what peccant humors[89] his patient naturally is most subject unto before he can begin his cure: I shall therefore shortly note unto you the principal faults that every rank of your people in this country is most subject unto. And as for England, I will speak be-gesse[90] of them, never having been among them, although I hope in that God who ever favors the right, before I die to be as well acquainted with their fashions.

As the whole subjects of our country (by the ancient and fundamental policy of our kingdom) are divided into three estates, so is every estate hereof generally subject to some special vices (which in a manner by long habitude) are thought rather virtue nor vice among them: not that every particular man in any of these ranks of men is subject unto them, *Nam nulla regula tam generalis quae non patiatur exceptionem,*[91] But that I mean, I have found by experience, these vices to have taken greatest hold with these ranks of men.

And first, that I prejudge not the Church of her ancient privileges, reason would she should have the first place (for order's sake) in this catalog.

The natural sicknesses that have ever troubled and been the decay of all the churches since the beginning of the world, changing the candlestick from one to another (as John says)[92] have been pride, ambition, an avarice. And now last, these

---

[89]**peccant humors** According to the medical theory of the time many diseases were caused by too much peccant humor which aggravated the tissues and possibly caused internal fermentation and/or reacted badly with the body's other humors.

[90]**be-gesse** at a guess, at random

[91]**Nam...exceptionem** *In fact, there is no general rule that does not permit of some exception.* legal maxim

[92] Rev 2:5 "Remember therefore from whence thou art fallen, and repent,

same infirmities wrought the overthrow of the Popeish Church in this country and divers others. But the Reformation of religion in Scotland being made by a popular tumult and rebellion (as well appeared by the destruction of our policy) and not proceeding from the prince's order (as it did in England) some of our fiery ministers got such a guiding of the people at that time of confusion, as finding the gust[93] of government sweet, they begouth[94] to fantasy to themselves a democratic form of government; and having (by the iniquity of the time) been over-well baited upon the wrack, first of my grandmother,[95] and syne of my own mother;[96] and after usurping the liberty of the time in my long minority, settled themselves so fast upon that imagined democracy, as they fed themselves with that home to become *tribuni plebis:*[97] and so in a popular government by leading the people by the nose, to bear the sway of all the rule. And for this cause, there never rose faction in the time of my minority, nor trouble sensyne,[98] but they were ever upon the wrong end of it; quarreling me not for any evil vice in me, but because I was a king, which they thought the highest evil: and because they were ashamed to profess this quarrel, they were busy to look narrowly in all my actions; and I warrant you a moat in my eye, yes, a false report was matter enough for them to work upon: and yet (for all their cunning) some of them would whiles snapper out well grossly[99] with the truth of their intentions; informing the people that all kings and princes were naturally enemies to the liberty of the church, and could never patiently bear

---

and do the first workes: or els I wil come against thee shortly, and wil remove they candlesticke out of his place, except thou amende."
[93] **gust** taste
[94] **begouth** began
[95] Mary of Guise a.k.a. Mary of Lorraine (1538–1560)
[96] Mary Stuart, Queen of Scots (1542–1587)
[97] **tribuni plebis** *people's tribunes* branch of the Roman government that represented the common people and had the power to veto legislation.
[98] **sensyne** since then
[99] **snapper out well grossly** be quick to find big faults

the yoke of Christ (with such sound doctrine fed they their flock) And because there was ever some learned and honest men of the ministry, that were ashamed of the presumption of these seditious people, there could be no way found out so meet for maintaining their plots, as Parity in the Church:[100] whereby the ignorant were emboldened (as bairdes)[101] to cry the learned, godly, and modest out of it; Parity, the mother of confusion and enemy to unity, which is the mother of odor; by the example whereof in the ecclesiastical government, they think (with time) to draw the politic and civil government to the like. Take heed therefore (my son) to these Puritans, very pests in the church and commonweal of Scotland; whom (by long experience) I have found, no deserts can oblige, oaths nor promises bind, breathing nothing but sedition and calumnies aspiring without measure, railing without reason, and making their own imaginations (without any warrant of the word) the square of their conscience. I protest before the great God (and since I am here upon my testament, it is no place for me to lie in) that I never found with any Highland or Border thieves so great ingratitude, and so many lies and vile perjuries, as I have found with some of them; and suffer not the principals of them to brook[102] you land if you like to sit at rest: except

---

[100]**Parity in the Church** A fundamental tenant of Presbyterianism that holds that all clergymen have equal rank in the church and that important decisions should be voted on by assemblies rather than handed down by a bishop. During the later part of his residence in Scotland James embarked on a series of actions intended to weaken the practical implications of Parity—both to curb the unruly Presbyterian faction and to smooth relations with the Church of England, which was (and is) organized on an Episcopal system. Those policies worked by restoring some of the prestige that Scots bishops had lost during the Reformation: naming bishops as "moderators" of the General Assembly and repealing the Act of Annexation so bishops could again administer income producing properties, and convening the General Assembly at times and places where fewer of the poorer clergy would be able to attend.
[101]**bairdes** poets (bards); mockers or lampooners
[102]**brook** use or enjoy

you would keep them for trying your patience, as Socrates did an evil wife:[103] and for preservative against their poison, entertain and advance the godly learned, and modest men of the ministry, whom of (God be praised) there lacks not a reasonable number: And by their preferment to bishoprics and benefices (annulling that vile Act of Annexation[104] if you find it not done to your hand) you shall not only banish their Parity (which can not agree with a monarchy) but you shall also reestablish the old institution of three estates in Parliament, which can no otherwise be done: but in this I hope (if God spare me days) to make you a fair entry; always where I leave, follow you my footsteps: and the first that rails against you, punish with the rigor of the law; for I have else in my days burst them with over-much reason.

And to end my advice anent the church state, cherish no man more than a good pastor: hate no man more than a proud Puritan, thinking it one of your fairest styles, to be called a loving nourish-father[105] to the Church, seeing all the churches within your dominions planted with good pastors: the doctrine and discipline maintained in purity according to God's word, a sufficient provision for their sustentation; a comely odor in their policy: pride punished, humility advanced: and they so to reverence their superiors, and their flocks them, as the flourishing of your church in piety, peace and learning, may be one of the chief points of your earthly glory, being ever alike war with both the extremities, as well as you repress the vain

---

[103]This is a reference to Xenophon's *Symposium*. The story is also repeated in Plutarch's *Moralia*. Allusions to Xanthippe's shrewishness were frequent in Elizabethan popular culture (q.v. Shakespeare's *Taming of the Shrew* Act I Scene 2 Line 71).

[104]**Act of Annexation** (1587) Seized property from the Church. It was intended as a way to replenish the treasury, which had been depleted during the regency. It was fairly unpopular and James came to believe that the money received had not been worth the damage to what we would now call "public relations."

[105]**nourish-father** nurturing father. q.v. *Acts Jas. VI. 1609* in which James refers to himself as "the nuris-father of the Kirk."

Puritan, so not to suffer proud papal bishops: but as some for their qualities will deserve to be preferred before others, so chain them with such bonds as my preserve that estate from creeping to corruption.

The next estate now by order comes in purpose, according to their ranks in parliament, is the nobility, although second in rank, yet over-far first in greatness and power, either to do good or evil as they are inclined.

The natural sicknesses that I have perceived this estate subject to in my time, hath been, a feckless arrogant conceit of their greatness and power: drinking in with their very nourish-milk,[106] that their honor stood in committing three points of iniquity: to thrall[107] (by oppression) the meaner sort that dwells near them to their service and following, although they hold nothing of them: to maintain their servants and dependers[108] in any wrong, although they be not answerable to the laws (for anybody will maintain his man in a right cause): and for any displeasure that they apprehend to be done unto them by their neighbor, to take up a plain feud against him, and (without respect to God, king, or commonweal) to bang it out bravely, he and all his kin against him and all his: yes they will think the king far in their common, in case they agree to grant an assurance to a short day for keeping of the peace: where, by their natural duty, they are obliged to obey the law and keep the peace all the days of their life, upon the peril of their craiges.[109]

For remedy to these evils in their estate, learn your nobility to keep your laws as precisely as the meanest: fear not their orping[110] nor taking the pet[111] as long as you rule well; for their pretended reformation of princes takes never effect,

---

[106] **nourish-milk** nurse's milk
[107] **thrall** enslave
[108] **dependers** followers, dependents
[109] **craiges** necks or throats
[110] **orping** fretting, repining
[111] **taking the pet** taking offense, being in a bad humor

but where evil government precedes. Acquaint your self so with all the honest men of your barons and gentlemen, as may make them perte[112] to make their own suits to you themselves, without making a boggle[113] of you, in making the great lords their intercessors (for intercession to saints is Papistry) so shall you bring to a measure their monstrous backs. And for their barbarous feuds, put the laws to due execution made by me thereanents,[114] beginning ever rathest[115] at him that you love best and is most obliged unto you, to make him an example to the rest; for you shall make all your reformations to begin at your elbow, and so by degrees to flow to the extremities of the land, and rest not while you root out these barbarous feuds, that their effects may as well be smoared down,[116] as their barbarous name is unknown to any other nations: for if this treatise were written to you, either in French or Latin, I could not get them named unto you but by circumlocution:[117] and for your easier abolishing of them, put sharply to execution my laws made against guns and traitorous pistolettes,[118] thinking in your heart, terming in your speech, and using by your punishments all such as wear and use them, as brigands and cutthroats.

On the other part, eschew the other extremity, in lighly-

---

[112]**perte** brisk, lively, smart

[113]**boggle** shadow, goblin, specter

[114]**thereanents** thereabouts

[115]**rathest** fastest; most savagely

[116]**smoared down** smothered, suffocated

[117]The meaning of this sentence is unclear, since both French and Latin contain ample vocabulary for describing feuding nobles.

[118]In the Elizabethan period the most common infantry firearm was still the match-lock harquebuss. Wheel-lock pistols were large and relatively cumbersome weapons, intended for cavalry and navel service, with a heavy barrel that allowed them to double as clubs. "Pistolettes," pistols small enough to be concealed under clothing, were rare and would have been cost prohibitive for any except the nobility. The distinctive "Highland" type pistol did not appear until at least a generation later.

ing[119] and contemning your nobility: Remember how that error broke the king my grandfather's[120] heart: but consider that virtue follows oftest noble blood. The worthiness of their antecessors craves a reverent regard to be had unto them: honor them therefore that are obedient to the law among them, as peers and fathers of your land. The frequentlier that your court can be garnished with them, think it the more honor, acquainting and employing them in all your greatest affairs, since it is they must be your arms and executors of your laws, and so use yourself lovingly to the obedient, and rigorously to the stubborn, as may make the greatest of them to think, that the chiefest point of their honor stands in striving with the meanest of the land in humility towards you, and obedience to your laws: dinging ever in their ears, that one of the principal points of service that you crave of them is, in their persons to practice, and by their power to procure due obedience to the law; without the which, no service they can make can be agreeable unto you.

But the greatest hinder to the execution of our law in this country, are the heritable sheriffdoms and regalities,[121] which being in the hands of the great men wrack the whole country: for which I know no present remedy, but by taking the sharper account of them in their offices, using all punishment against the slothful that the law will permit: and aye as they vaik[122] for any offenses committed by them, dispone[123] them never heritable again: preassing (with time) to draw it to the

---

[119]**lighlying** underestimating, speaking lightly of
[120]James IV (1473–1513)
[121]In Scotland both of these were crown offices that gave the holder jurisdiction to investigate and try crimes within their their territory. Of the two, a "Lord of Regality" was more powerful, being competent to try any offense against the crown, while a Sheriff was competent only to try murder, but both offices came with considerable police powers.
[122]**vaik** become vacant
[123]**dispone** revise legally

lowable[124] custom of England, which you may the easily do being king of both, as I hope in God you shall.

And as for the third and last estate, which is the burghs[125] (for the small barons are but an inferior part of the nobility and of their estate) the burghs (I say) are composed of two sorts of men; to wit, merchants and craftsmen,[126] every one of these sorts being subject to their own infirmities.

The merchants think the whole commonweal ordained for making them up, and (accounting it their lawful gain and trade, to enrich themselves upon the loss of all the rest of the people) they transport from us things necessary, bringing back whiles unnecessary and whiles nothing. They buy for us the worst wares, and sell them at the dearest prices: and suppose the victuals fall or rise of their prices, (according to the abundance or scantness thereof) yet the prices of their wares ever rise but never fall according to the Persian laws that can not be abrogated: and they are the special cause of the corruption of the coinzie,[127] transporting all our own and bringing in foreign, upon what price they please to set on it. For order putting to them, put good laws in execution that are already made anent these abuses: but especially do three things: establish honest, diligent, but few searchers, (for many hands make slight work)[128] and have an honest and diligent treasurer to take count of them: permit and allure foreign merchants, to trade here, so shall you have best and best cheap wares, not buying it at the third hand: and set every year down a certain price for all things, confiding first, how it is in other countries, and the price being set reasonably down, if the merchants will not bring it home on the price, cry foreigners free to bring it.

And because I have made mention here of the coinzie, make

---

[124]**lowable** laudable, commendable
[125]**burghs** chartered towns
[126]Peasants and casual laborers, of course, had no voice in the government and so, presumably, did not need to be considered in this section.
[127]**coinzie** coin
[128]Proverbial

your coinzie fine gold and silver, and garre[129] the people be payed with substance, and not abused with number; so shall you enrich the commonweal, and keep a great pose[130] to the fore, if you fall in wars or in any straits, for the making it baser will breed your commodity, but it is not to be used but at a great necessity.

And the craftsmen think we should be content with their work, how bad and dear so ever it be; and (if they in anything be controlled) up must the Blue Blanket[131] go; but for their part take example by England, how it hath flourished both in wealth and policy, since the strangers' craftsmen came in among them. Therefore not only permit, but allure strangers to come here also, taking as straight order for repressing the mutinying of ours at them, as was done in England at their first in-bringing there.

But unto one fault is all the common people of this land subject as well burgh as land, which is, to judge and speak rashly of their prince, setting the commonweal upon four props, (as we call it) ever wearying of the present estate, and desirous of novelties: for remedy whereof (besides the execution of laws that would be used against unreverent speakers) certain days in the year would be appointed, for delighting the people with public spectacles of all honest games and exercise of arms, as also for convening of neighbors for entertaining friendship and hartlinesse,[132] by honest feasting and merriness: for I cannot see what greater superstition can be in making plays and lawful games in May, and good cheer at Yule, than in eating fish in Lentron[133] and upon Fridays, the Papists as well using the one as the other, so that always the sabbath be kept holy, and

---

[129]**garre** cause or force
[130]**pose** a hoard or hidden treasure
[131]**Blue Blanket** traditional banner of the craftsmen of Edinburgh since the time of James III.
[132]**hartlinesse** cordiality, warmth of heart
[133]**Lentron** Lent

no unlawful sports used: and this form of alluring the people, hath been used in all well governed republics.

You see now (my son) how (for the zeal I bear to acquaint you with the plain and single verity of all things) I have not spared to play the bairde against all the estates of my kingdom; but I protest before God, I do it with the fatherly love that I owe to them all, only hating their vices, whereof there is a good number of honest men free in every estate.

And because (for the better reformation of all these abuses among your estates) it will be a great help unto you, to be well acquainted with the nature and humors of all your subjects, and to know particularly the estate of every part of your dominions; I would therefore counsel you, once in the year to visit the principal parts of the country you were in; and (because I hope you shall be king of more countries than this) once in three years to vise all your kingdoms, not lippening[134] to viceroys but hearing yourself their complaints, and having ordinary counsels and justice seats in every kingdom of their own countrymen, and the principal matters ever to be decided by yourself when you come athwart.

You have also to consider, that you must not only be careful to keep your subjects from receiving any wrong of others within, but also you must be careful to keep them from the wrong of any foreign prince without, since the sword is given you by God, not only to revenge upon your own subjects the wrongs committed upon others, but further, to revenge and free them of foreign injuries done unto them: and therefore wars upon just quarrels are lawful: but above all, let not the wrong cause be on your side.

Use all other princes (as your brethren) honestly and kindly, keep precisely your promise unto them, although with your hurt: strive with every one of them in courtesy and thankfulness; as with all men, so especially with them be plain and truthful, keeping ever that Christian rule: to do as you would

---

[134]**lippening** trusting

[39]

be done to—especially in counting rebellion against any other prince, a crime against yourself because of the preparative. Supply therefore, nor trust not other prince's rebels; but pity and succor all lawful princes in their troubles. But if any of them will not abstain (notwithstanding whatsoever your good deserts) to wrong you or your subjects, crave redress at leisure: hear and do all reason, and if no offer that is lawful or honorable, can make him abstain nor repair his wrongdoing then for last refuge, commit the justness of your cause to God, giving first honestly up with him, and in a public and honorable form.

But omitting now to teach you the form of making wars (because that art is better learned by practice nor speculation)[135] I will only set down to you here few precepts therein. Let first the justness of your cause be your greatest strength, and then omit not to use all lawful means for backing of the same. Consult therefore with no necromancer nor prophet upon the success of your wars: remembering on King Saul's miserable end.[136] But (since all prophecies are ceased in Christ) keep your land clean of all soothsayers, according to the command in the Law of God,[137] and dilated by Jeremy.[138] Neither commit your quarrel to be tried by a duel, for it is a committing of it to a lot, and there is no warrant for it in the scripture since the abrogating of the old law.

---

[135] James himself had extremely limited military experience.

[136] 1 Sam 31:4 "Then said Saul unto his armour bearer, Drawe out thy sworde, and thrust me through therewith, lest the uncircumcised come and thrust me through and mocke me: but his armour bearer wolde not, for he was sore afrayed. Therefore Saul toke a sworde and fel upon it."

[137] Deut 18:10 "Let none be founde among you that maketh his sonne or his daughter to go through the fire, or that useth witchcraft, or a regarder of times, or a marker of the flying of foules, or a sorcerer"

[138] Jer 29:8–9 "For thus saith the Lord of hostes the God of Israel, Let not your prophetes, & your sothesayers that be among you, deceive you, nether give eare to your dreames, which you dreame. For they prophecie you a lue in my Name: I have not sent them, saith the Lord."

BOOK II

Before you take on wars, play the wise king's part described by Christ: foreseeing how you may bear it out with all necessary provision; especially remember that money is *nervus belli*.[139] Chose old experienced captains, and young able soldiers. Be extremely straight and severe in discipline, as well for keeping of order, (which is as requisite as hardiness in the wars) for punishing of sloth, (which at a time may put the whole army in hazard) as likewise for repressing of mutinies (which in wars is wonderful dangerous:) and look to the Spaniard, whose great success in all his wars hath only come through straightness of discipline and order; for such errors may be committed in the wars as cannot be gotten mended again.

Be in your own person walkerise,[140] diligent, and painful,[141] using the advice of them that are most skillful in the craft, as you must do in all crafts. Be homely[142] with your soldiers as your companions for winning their hearts; extremely liberal, for then is no time for sparing. Be cold and foreseeing in devising, constant in your resolutions, and forward and quick in your executions. Fortify well your camp, and assail not rashly without an advantage. Neither fear nor lighly your enemies. Be curious[143] in devising stratagems (but always honestly) for of anything they work greatest effects in the wars, if secrecy be joined to invention. And once or twice in your own person hazard yourself fairly but (having acquired so the fame of courage and magnanimity) make not a daily soldier of yourself, exposing rashly your person to every peril, but conserve yourself thereafter for the weal of your people, for whose sake you must more care for yourself nor your own.

And as I have counseled you to be slow in taking on a

---

[139]**nervus belli** *[the] sinews of war* Proverbial. It appears in Cicero's *Fifth Philippic* but was probably in use by the time of the Peloponnesian Wars.

[140]**walkerise** watchful

[141]**painful** painstaking

[142]**homely** informal; plain spoken

[143]**curious** skillful, fastidious, particular

war, so advise I you to be slow in peacemaking. Before you agree, look that the ground of your wars be satisfied in your peace; and that you see a good surety for you and your people: otherwise, an honorable and just war is more tolerable than a dishonorable and disadvantageous peace.

But it is not enough to be a good king, by the thralldom[144] of good laws well executed to govern his people, if he join not therewith his virtuous life in his own person and in the person of his court and company, by his good example alluring his subjects to the love of virtue, and hatred of vice; And therefore (my son) since all people are naturally inclined to follow their prince's example (as I showed you before) let it not be said, that you command others to keep the contrary course to that which in your own person you practice, making so your words and deeds to fight together: but by the contrary, let your own life be a law book and a mirror to your people, that therein they may read the practice of their own laws; and therein they may see by your shadow what life they should lead.

And this example in your own life and person, I likewise divide in two parts: The first, in government of your court and followers in all godliness and virtue, the next, in having your own mind decked and enriched so with all virtuous qualities, that therewith you may worthily rule your people, for it is not enough that you have and retain (as prisoners) within yourself never so many good qualities and virtues, except you employ them and set them on work for the weal of them that are committed to your charge, *Omnis etenim virtus in actione consistit.*[145]

First then, as the government of your court and followers, as you ought to have a great care for the ruling well of all your subjects, so ought you to have a double care for the ruling well of your own servants, since unto them you are both a politic,

---

[144]**thralldom** slavery, bondage

[145]**Omnis... actione** *For indeed, all virtues consist of action.* from a Latin translation of Aristotle's *Nicomachean Ethics*

and economic governor; and as every one of the people will delight to follow the example of any of the courtiers, as well in evil as in good, so what crime so horrible can be committed and overseen in a courtier, that will be an exemplar excuse for any other of the people boldly to commit the like. And therefore, in two points you would take good heed anent your court and household: first, in choosing them wisely, next, in careful ruling them whom you have chosen.

It is an old and true proverb, that a kindly aver[146] will never become a good horse; for albeit good education and company be great helps to nature, *habitudo*[147] being most justly called *altera natura*,[148] yet is it evil to get out of the flesh what is bred in the bone (as the old proverb says:) be very ware then in making choice of your servants and company.

Nam turpis eicitur, quam non admititur hospes.[149]

And many respects may lawfully let an admission, that will not be sufficient causes of deprivation.

All your servants and court must be composed partly of minors (such as young lords to be brought up in your company, or pages and such like) and partly of men of perfite age, for serving you in such rooms as ought to be filled with men of wisdom and discretion. For the first sort, you can do no more but choose them within age, that are come of a good and virtuous kind, *in fide parentum*[150] as baptism is used: for suppose that *anima non venit ex traduce*,[151] but is immediately created by God and infused from above; yes it is most certain, that virtue or vice will ofttimes (with the heritage)

---

[146]**aver** cart horse

[147]**habitudo** *condition; habit*

[148]**altera natura** *other nature*

[149]**Nam...hospes** *For you shall banish evil by not admitting foreigners/enemies.*

[150]**in fide parentum** *in the manner of a faithful parent*

[151]**anima...traduce** *[the] soul is not passed across [from the parents]*

be transferred from the parents to the posterity, and run on a blood (as the proverb is) the sickness of the mind becoming as kindly to some races, as these sicknesses of the body that smites in the seed. Especially choose such minors as are come of a true and honest race, and have not had the house whereof the are descended infected with falsehood.

And as for the other sort of your company and servants that ought to be of perfite age: first see that they be of a good fame and without blemish; otherwise, what can people think? But that you have chosen a company unto you according to your own humor, and so have preferred these men for the love of their vices and crimes that you know them to be guilty of: for the people that see you not within, can not judge of you but according to the outward appearance of your actions and company, which is subject to their fight. And next, see that they be endued with such honest qualities, as are meet for such offices as you ordain them to serve in, that your judgment may be known in employing every man according to his gifts; and shortly, follow good King David's counsel in the choice of your servants, by setting your eye upon the faithful and upright of the land to dwell with you.[152]

But here I must not forget to remember, and (according to my fatherly authority) to charge you to prefer specially to your service so many as have truly served me, and are able for it; the rest, honorably to reward them, preferring their posterity before others as kindliest: so shall you not only be best served, (for if the haters of your parents can not love you (as I showed before) it follows of necessity their lovers must love you)[153] but further, you shall kithe your thankful memory of your father, and procure the blessing of their old master in you, which

---

[152]The reference is somewhat unclear, but is likely a gloss on Ps 101:6–7, "Mine eies shalbe unto the faithful of the land, that they maie dwell with me: he that walketh in a perfite waie, he shal serve me. There shal no deceitful persone dwell within mine house: he that telleth lies, shal not remaine in my sight."

[153]It does not; this is a logical *non sequitor*.

otherwise would be turned in a prayer for me and a curse for you. Use them therefore after my death as the testimonies of your affection towards me; trusting and advancing those farthest whom I found faithfulest: which you must discern not by their rewards, at my hand (for rewards, as they are *bona Fortunae*,[154] so are they subject unto Fortune) but according to the trust I gave them, having oft-times had better heart than happe[155] to the rewarding of sundry: And on the other part, as I wish you to kithe your constant love towards them that I loved, so desire I you to kithe in the same measure your constant hatred to them that I hated; I mean bring not home, nor restore not such as you find standing banished or forefalted by me: The contrary would kithe in you over-great a contempt of me, and lightness in your own nature; For how can they be true to the son that were false to the father?

But to return to the purpose anent the choice of your servants, you shall by this wise form of doing eschew the inconvenience that in my minority I fell in anent the choice of my servants: for by they that had the command where I was brought up were my servants put unto me, not choosing them that were meetest to serve me, but whom they thought meetest to serve their turn about me—as kithed well in many of them at the first rebellion raised against me; which compelled me to make a great alteration among my servants: and yet the example of that corruption made me to be long troubled thereafter with solicitors, recommending servants unto me more for serving in effect their master that admitted them. Let my example then teach you to follow the rules here set down, choosing your servants for your own use, and not for the use of others: and since you must be *communis aura*[156] to all your people, so chose your servants indifferently out of all quarters, not respecting other men's appetites, but their own qualities: for as you must com-

---

[154]**bona Fortunae** *good Fortune*
[155]**happe** *good luck*
[156]**communis aura** *[the] public breath*

mand all, so reason would you should be served out of all as you please to make choice. But specially take good heed to the choice of your servants that you prefer to the offices of the crown and estate;[157] for in other offices you have only to take heed to your own weal, but these concern likewise the weal of your people for the which you must be answerable to God. Choose then for all these offices men of known wisdom, honesty, and good conscience, well practiced in the points of the craft that you ordain them for, and free of all factions and partialities: preferring them (as you will be answerable to God) only for their worthiness, and not for pleasing of friends: but specially choose honest, diligent, mean (but responsible) men to be your receivers in money matters: mean (I say) that you may when you please take a sharp account of their intromission,[158] without peril of their brewing any trouble to your estate: for this hath bin the greatest wight[159] of my misthriving in money matters: especially, put never a foreigner in any principal office of estate, for that will never fail to stir up sedition and envy in the countrymen's hearts both against you and him. But (as I said before) if God provide you with more countries than this, chose the born-men of every country to be your chief counselors therein: And for conclusion of my advice anent the choice of your servants, delight to be served with men of the noblest blood that can be had: for besides that their service shall breed you great goodwill, and least envy (contrary to that of start-ups) you shall oft find virtue follow noble races, (as I have said before speaking of the nobility).

Now, as to the other point, anent your governing of your servants when you have chosen them: make your court and company to be a pattern of godliness and all honest virtues to all the rest of the people; be a daily watchman over your

[157]**crown and estate** In modern terminology, *crown* officers would be executive branch appointees, whereas *estate* officers would be the Stuarts' own household employees.
[158]**intromission** legal term for act of meddling with another's property
[159]**wight** creator, maker

servants, that they obey your laws precisely (for how can your
laws be kept in the country, if they be broken at your lugg?)[160]
punishing the breach thereof in a courtier, more severely than
in the person of any other of your subjects; and above all,
suffer none of them (by abusing their credit with you) to op-
press or wrong any of your subjects. Be homely or strange[161]
with them as you think their behavior deserve, and their nature may bear with. Think a querulous man a pest in your
company: be careful ever to prefer the gentlest natured and
trustiest to the inwardest[162] offices about you, especially in
your chamber. Suffer none about you to mell[163] in any men's
particulars, but like the Turk's Janissairs,[164] let them know no
father but you, nor particular but yours: And if any will mell
in their kin or friends' quarrels, give him his leave; for since
you must be of no surname nor kin, but equal to all honest
men, it becomes you not to be followed with partial or fac-
tious servants. Teach obedience to your servants, and not to
think themselves over-wise; and (as when any of them deserve
it) you must not spare to put them away; so, without a seen
cause change none of them. Pay them (as all others your subjects) with *praemium* or *poena*[165] as they deserve, which is the
very ground-stone of good government; Employ every man as
you think him qualified, but use not one in all things, least
he wax proud and be envied by his marrowes.[166] Love them
best that are plainest with you, and disguise not the truth for
all their kin. Suffer none to be evil tongued nor backbiters of

---

[160]**lugg** ear
[161]**homely or strange** familiar or distant
[162]**inwardest** most intimate
[163]**mell** involve oneself with
[164]**Janissairs** Janissaries. From the 14th through 19th centuries, the elite infantry corps of the Ottoman Empire. They were famous for their iron discipline and their training, which began early in boyhood. Both the discipline and quality of training had begun to decline by James' time, but the Janissaries were still formidable soldiers.
[165]**praemium** or **poena** *recompense* or *fine*
[166]**marrowes** mates, companions

them they hate: Command a hartly and brotherly love among all them that serve you: and shortly, maintain peace in your court and banish envy; cherish modesty, banish debouched insolence; foster humility, repress pride; setting down such a comely and honorable order in all the points of your service, that when strangers shall visit your court, they may (with the Queen of Sheba)[167] admire your wisdom in the glory of your house, and comely order among your servants.

But the principal blessing that you can get of good company will stand in your marrying of a godly and virtuous wife, for she must be nearer unto you than any other company, being flesh of your flesh and bone of your bone (as God himself said to Adam).[168] and because I know not but God may call me before you be ready for marriage, I will shortly set down to you here my advice therein.

First of all consider that marriage is the greatest earthly felicity or misery that can come to a man, according as it pleases God to bless or curse the same: since without the blessing of God then you cannot look for a happy success in marriage, you must be careful both in your preparation for it, and in the choice and usage of your wife to procure the same. By your preparation I mean that you must keep your body clean and unpolluted, while you give it to your wife whomto only it belongs: for how can you justly crave to be joined with a pure virgin if your body be polluted? Why should the one half be clean and the other defiled? And suppose I know, fornication is thought but a venial sin by the most part of the world, yet remember well what I said to you in my first book anent

---

[167] 1 Kings 10:4–5 "Then the quene of Sheba sawe all Salomons wisdom, and the house that he had buylt and the meate of his table, and the fitting of his servants, and the ordre of his ministers, & there apparel, & his drinking vessels, and his burnt offrings, that he offred in the house of the Lord, and she was greatly astonied."

[168] Actually, Adam said it to God: Gen 2:23 "Then the man said, This is bone of my bones, and flesh of my flesh. She shalbe called woman, because she was taken out of man."

conscience, and count every sin and breach of God's law, not according as the vain world esteems of it, but as God the judge and maker the law accounts the same: hear God commanding by the mouth of Paul[169] to abstain from fornication, declaring that the fornicator shall not inherit the kingdom of heaven; and by the mouth of John[170] reckoning out fornication among other grievous sins that debars the committers among dogs and sin, from entry in that spiritual and heavenly Jerusalem: and consider, if a man shall once take upon him to count that light which God calls heavy, and venial that God calls grievous beginning first to measure any one sin by the rule of his lust and appetites, and not of his conscience. What shall let him to do so with the next that his affections shall stir him to, the like reason serving for all? And so to go forward while he place his whole corrupted affections in God's room, and then what shall come of him? But (as a man given over to his own filthy affections) shall perish into them. And because we are all of that nature, that sibbest[171] examples twicheth[172] us nearest, consider the difference of success that God granted in the marriages of the king my grandfather[173] and me your own father the reward of his harlotry (proceeding from his evil education) being the sudden death at one time of two pleasant young princes; and a daughter only born to succeed to him whom he had never the happe so much as once to see or bless before his death, leaving a double curse behind him to the land, both a woman of sex, and a new born babe of age to reign over them: And as for the reward of my continence, your-

---

[169]1 Cor 6:9–10 "Knowe ye not that the unrighteous shal not inherite the kingdome of God? Be not deceived: nether fornicators, nor idolaters, nor adulterers, nor wantons, nor bouggerers, nor theves, nor covetous, nor drunkards, nor railers, nor extorcioners shal inherite the kingdome of God."

[170]Rev 22:15 "For without shalbe dogges & enchanters, & whoremongers, & mutherers, & idolaters, & whosoever loveth or maketh lyes."

[171]**sibbest** kindred; nearly related; like

[172]**twicheth** touch

[173]James V of Scotland (1512–1542)

self and sibbe-folkes[174] to you are (praise be to God) sufficient witnesses.

Be not ashamed then to keep clean your body (which is the temple of the holy spirit[175] notwithstanding all vain allurements to the contrary, discerning truly and wisely of every virtue and vice according to the true qualities thereof, and not according to the vain conceits of men.

As for your choice in marriage, respect chiefly the three causes wherefore marriage was first ordained by God, and then join three accessories, so far as they may be obtained underogating[176] to the principles.

The three causes it was ordained for are for staying of lust, for procreation of children, and that man should by his wife get a helper like himself. Defer not then to marry while your age, for it is ordained for staunching the lust in your youth. Especially a king must timously marry for the weal of his people, nor marry not (for any accessory cause or worldly respects) a woman unable either through age, nature, or accident, for procreation of children; for in a king that were a double fault as well against his own weal as against the weal of his people. Nor yet marry one of known evil conditions nor vicious education,[177] for the woman is ordained to be a helper and not a hinderer to man.

The three accessories which (as I have said) ought also to be respected without underogating to the principal causes; are beauty, riches, and friendship by allie,[178] which are all blessings of God: for beauty increases your love to your wife,

---

[174]**sibbe-folks** blood relatives. In this case, specifically Elizabeth and Charles.

[175]1 Cor 6:19 "Know ye not, that your bodie is the temple of the holie Gost, which is in you, whome ye have of God? And ye are not your owne."

[176]**underogating** not detracting from

[177]The 1887 text reads "nor yet marry *not* one of known evil conditions or vicious education" but the double negative does not seem to make sense in this context.

[178]**allie** alliance

contenting you the better with her without care for others:
and riches and great allie, do both make her the abler to be
a helper unto you: but if (over-great respect being had to
these accessories) the principal causes be over-seen (which is
oft-practiced in the world) as of themselves they are a blessing
being well used, so the abuse of them will turn them in a curse:
for what can all these worldly respects avail, when a man shall
find himself coupled with a devil, to be one flesh with him and
the half marrowe in his bed? Then (though too late) shall he
find that beauty without bounty, wealth without wisdom, and
great friendship without grace and honesty, are but fair shows
and the deceitful masques of infinite miseries.

But have you respect (my son) to yon three special causes
in your marriage, which flow from the first institution thereof.[179]
Et caetera omnia adiicientur vobis:[180] and therefore beware to
marry any but one of your own religion: for how can you be of
one flesh and keep unity betwixt you, being members of two
opposite churches? Disagreement in religion brings ever with
it disagreement in manners, and the dissension betwixt your
preachers and hers will breed and foster a dissension among
your subjects, taking their example from your family, besides
the peril of the evil education of your children. Neither pride
you that you will be able to frame and make her as you please;
that deceived Solomon, the wisest king that ever was,[181] the
grace of perseverance not being a flower that grows in our
garden. Remember also that marriage is one of the greatest
actions that a man does in all his time, especially in taking
his first wife; and if he marry first basely beneath his rank,
he will ever be the less accounted of thereafter. And lastly,
remember to choose your wife as I advised you to choose your
servants, that she be of a whole and clean race, not subject to

---

[179]Mt 6:33 "But seke ye first the kingdome of God, and his righteousnes,
& all these things shalbe ministered unto you."

[180]**Et...vobis** *And all the rest will be added onto you.* Probably a paraphrase
from Mat. 6:33

[181]1 Kings 11:1–8

the hereditary sicknesses, either of the soul or the body. For if a man will be careful to breed horses and dogs of good kinds, how much more careful should he be for the breed of his own loins? So shall you in your marriage have respect to your conscience, honor, and natural weal in your successors. When you are married, keep inviolably your promise made to God in your marriage, which all stands in doing of one thing, and abstaining from another, to treat her in all things as your wife and the half of yourself, and to make your body (which then is no more yours but properly hers) common with none other. I trust I need not to insist here to dissuade you from the filthy vice of adultery; remember only what solemn promise you make to God at your marriage, and since it is only by the force of that promise that your bairnes[182] succeed unto you, which otherwise they could not do. Equity and reason would you should keep your part thereof. God is ever a severe avenger of all perjuries; and it is no oath made in mowes, that gives power to bairnes to succeed to great kingdoms. Have the king my grandfather's[183] example before your eyes, who by his adultery bred the wrak[184] of his lawful daughter and heir, in begetting that bastard[185] who unnaturally rebelled and procured the ruin of his own sister: and what good her posterity has gotten sensyne of that unlawful generation, Bothwell's[186] tricks can bear

---

[182]**bairnes** children

[183]James V of Scotland (1513–1542)

[184]**wrak** ruin

[185]James Stuart, Earl of Murray (c.1531–1570), natural son of James V through Margaret Erskine. One of the chief power players and intriguers of the country throughout Mary's reign, and later the first of James VI's four regents. While he was indisputably involved in forcing Mary's abdication, he may also have tried to protect her life from Elizabeth I and from more radical elements of his own faction.

[186]James Hepburn, 4th Earl of Bothwell (c.1536–1578), who was implicated in a plot to assassinate Mary's husband Henry Stuart, Lord Darnley and widely believed to have been her extramarital lover (although the authenticity of the key evidence in the later accusation, the so called "Casket Letters", continues to be debated). After Darnley's

witness. Keep precisely then your promise made at marriage, as you would wish to be partaker of the blessing therein. And for your behavior to your wife, the scripture can best give you counsel therein: Treat her as your own flesh. Command her as her lord. Cherish her as your helper. Rule her as your pupil. Please her in all things reasonable, but teach her not to be curious in things that belongs her not; you are the head, she is your body. It is your office to command and hers to obey; but yet with such a sweet harmony, as she should be as ready to obey as you to command, as willing to follow as you to go before, your love being wholly knit unto her, and all her affections lovingly bent to follow your will. And to conclude, keep specially three rules with your wife: First, suffer her never to meddle with the politic government of the commonweal, but hold her at the economic rule of the house, and yet all to be subject to your direction: keep carefully good and chaste company about her, for women are the frailest sex And be never both angry at once, for when you see her in passion you should with reason dantone yours; for both when you are settled you are meetest to judge of her errors, and when she is come to her self, she may be best made to apprehend her offense and reverence your rebuke. If God send you succession, be careful for their virtuous education: love them as you ought, but let them know as much of it as the gentleness of their nature will deserve, containing them ever in a reverent love and loving fear of you: And in case it please God to provide you to all these three kingdoms,[187] make your eldest son Isaac, leaving him all your kingdoms, and provide the rest with private possessions.[188] Otherwise by dividing your kingdoms, you shall leave the seed of division and discord among your posterity; but if God give you not succession, defraud never the nearest by right, what ever conceit you have of the person: for king-

death they were married, alienating most of Mary's remaining political supporters. Bothwell fled Scotland in 1577 and never returned.
[187]Scotland, England and Ireland
[188]Gen 21:9–13

doms are ever at God's disposition, and in that case we are but liverentars,[189] lying no more in the king's nor peoples hands to dispossess the righteous heir.

And as your company should be a pattern to the rest of your people, so should your person be a lamp and mirror to your company, giving light to your servants to walk in the path of virtue, and representing unto them such worthy qualities as they should preasse to imitate.

I need not to trouble you with the particular discourse of the four cardinal virtues,[190] it is so trodden a path, but I will shortly say unto you: make one of them (which is temperance) queen of all the rest within you. I mean not by the vulgar interpretation of temperance, which only stands in the moderate using of meat and drink; but I mean of that wise moderation, that first commanding yourself, shall (as a queen) command all the affections and passions of your mind, and (as a physician) wisely mix all your actions according thereto. Therefore (not only in all your affections and passions, but) even in your most virtuous actions, make ever moderation to be the chief ruler. For although holiness be the first, and most requisite quality of a Christian (as proceeding from the true fear and knowledge of God) yet you remember how in the conclusion of my first book, I advised you to moderate all your outward actions flowing therefrom. The like say I now of justice, which is the greatest virtue that properly belongs to a king's office.

Use justice, but with such moderation as it turn not in tyranny, otherwise *summum jus*, is *summa injuria*.[191] As for example, if a man of a known honest life be invaded by brigands or thieves for his purse, and in his own defense slay one of them, because they were not at the horne, and that although they were both more in number, and also known to be

---

[189] **liverentars** tenants

[190] prudence, courage, temperance, and justice

[191] **summum jus, is summa injuria** *[The] total of law* is *[the] total of damages.* That is, do not impose sentences stricter than those required by the law. Cicero, *De Officiis*

debouched and insolent liars, where by the contrary, he was single alone, being a man of sound reputation; yet because there was no witness present that could verify their first invading of him, shall he therefore lose his head? and likewise by the law-burrows[192] in our laws, men are prohibited under pecunial, from any wise invading or molesting their neighbor's person or bounds; if then his horse break the tether and pastor in his neighbor's meadow, shall he pay two or three thousand pounds for the wantonness of his horse or the weakness of his tether? Surely no, for laws are ordained as rules of virtuous and social living, and not to be snares to trap your good subjects, and therefore the law must be interpreted according to the meaning, and not to the literal sense thereof, *Nam ratio est anima legis.*[193]

And as I said of justice, so say I of clemency, magnanimity, liberality, constancy, humility, and all other princely virtues, *Nam in medio fiat virtus.*[194] And it is but the craft of the Devil that falsely colors the two vices that are on either side thereof, with the borrowed titles thereof, albeit in very deed they have no affinity therewith: and the two extremities themselves, although they seem contrary, yet growing to the height run ever both in one: for what difference is betwixt extreme tyranny delighting to destroy all mankind; and extreme slackness of punishment, permitting every man to tyrannize over his marrow? And what differs extreme prodigality, by wasting of all to possess nothing; from extreme niggardness, by hoarding of all to enjoy nothing?[195] Like the ass that carrying victual on her back, is like to starve for hunger, and will be fain of;[196]

---

[192]**law-borrows** legal security posted by one person that he will not do personal or property injury to another
[193]**Nam... legis** *for reason is the soul of law* traditional legal maxim
[194]**Nam... virtus** *for virtue lies in the middle*
[195]cf. Dante's *Divine Comedy*, in which the fourth circle of hell is reserved for the avaricious and the prodigal (*Inferno, Canto VII*).
[196]**fain of** happy enough with

thistles for her part[197] and what is betwixt the pride of a glorious Nebuchadnezzar[198] and the preposterous humility of one of our Puritan ministers, claiming to their Parity, and crying, "we are all but vile worms," and yet will judge and give law to their king, but will be judged nor controlled by none: Surely, there is more pride under such a one's black bonnet, nor under great Alexander's diadem (as was said of the clouts of Diogenes).[199]

But above all virtues study to know well your own craft, which is to rule your people. And when I say this, I bid you know all crafts: For except you know every one, how can you control every one? Which is your proper office. Therefore, besides your education, it is necessary you delight in reading and seeking the knowledge of all lawful things, but with these two restrictions: first, that you choose idle hours for it, not interruption therewith the discharge of your office; and next, that you study not for knowledge nakedly, but that your principal end be, to make you able there by to use your office, practicing according to your knowledge in all the points of your calling not like those vain astrologians, that study night and day on the course of the stars, only that they may (for satisfying their curiosity) know their course. But since all arts and sciences are linked every one with other, their greatest principles agreeing in one (which moved poets to feign the nine muses to be all sisters) study them, that out of their harmony you may suck the knowledge of all faculties, and consequently, be on the counsel of all crafts, that you may be able to contain them all in order (as I have already said). Knowledge and learning is a light burden, the weight whereof will never press your shoulders: First

---

[197] Aesop's fable of *The Ass Eating Thistles*

[198] See the description of Nebuchadnezzar in the Bible's *Book* of *Daniel*.

[199] **clouts** clothing. Diogenes Lartius relates a meeting between Alexander and Diogenes in which Alexander introduced himself saying, "I am Alexander the great king", and Diogenes replied "And I am Diogenes the Cynic." On another occasion, also related by Plutarch, Diogenes told Alexander to move out of his sun.

of all then study to be well seen in the scriptures, as well for the knowledge of your own salvation, as that you may be able to contain your Church in their calling, as *custos utriusque tabulae*:[200] for the ruling them well is no small point of your office, taking specially heed, that they vague not from their text[201] in the pulpit. But snibbe sickerlie[202] the first that mints[203] to it; And (if he like to appeal or decline) when you have taken order with his head, his brethren may (if you please) powle his hair and pare his nails,[204] as the king my grandfather[205] said of a priest. Do nothing towards them without a good ground and warrant, but reason not much with them, for (as I have told you before) I have else over-much bursten[206] them with that, *Contra verbosos, noli contendere verbis.*[207] And suffer no conventions nor meetings among churchmen, but by your knowledge and permission.

Next the scriptures, study well your own laws: for how can you discern by the things you know not; but preasse to draw all your laws and processes to be as short and plain as you can: assure yourself, the longsomeness both of rights and processes, breeds their unsure looseness and obscurity, the shortest being ever both the surest and plainest form, and the longsomeness serves only for the enriching of the advocates and clerks with the spoil of the whole country. And therefore delight to haunt whiles your session, and spie[208] carefully their pro-

---

[200]**custos tabulae** *keeper/guardian of both tablets.* i.e. enforcer of the laws of both church and state, after the two tablets of the ten commandments.

[201]**vauge not from their text** stray from preaching on purely religious matters

[202]**snibbe sickerlie** check, hinder, reproach

[203]**mints** tries, attempts

[204]**powle his hair and pare his nails** cut his hair and nails

[205]James V of Scotland (1513–1542 CE)

[206]**bursten** burst; overpowered

[207]**Contra…verbis** *Against verbosity, don't contend with words.* Catonis Disticha, Dionysus Cato

[208]**spie** observe

ceedings, taking narrow tente[209] if any bribery be tried among them, which cannot over-severely be punished. Spare not to go there, for gracing (that far) any that you favor, by your presence to procure them expedition of justice (although that should be specially done for the poor that can no wait on) but when you are there, remember the throne is God's and not yours, that you sit in, and let no favor, nor whatsoever respects move you from the right; you sit not there (as I shewed before) for rewarding of friends or servants, not for crossing of condemners; but only for doing of justice. Learn also wisely to discern, betwixt justice and equity: for pity of the poor then, rob not the rich, because he may better spare it; but give the little man the most cloak, if it be his; eschewing the error of young Cyrus therein[210] for justice (by the law) gives every man his own: and equity in things arbitral,[211] gives every one that which is meetest for him.

Be an ordinary sitter in your secret counsel: that judicature is only ordained for matters of estate and repressing of insolent oppressions. Make that judgment as compendious and plain as you can, and suffer no advocates to be heard there with their delatoures,[212] but let every party tell his own tale himself; and weary not to hear the complaints of the oppressed, *aut ne rex sis?*[213] Remit every thing to the ordinary judicature for eschewing of confusion, but let it be your own craft to take a sharp account of every man in his office.

And next the laws, I would have you be well versed in authentic histories and specially in the chronicles of all nations. I mean not of such infamous invectives as Buchanan's[214] or

---

[209] **taking narrow tente** observing carefully
[210] Xenophon, *Cyropaedia*, I:3:16–17
[211] **arbitral** of or pertaining to arbiters; subject to the exercise of will
[212] **delatoures** accusers
[213] *for are you [not] a king?*
[214] **Buchanan** George Buchanan (1506–1582), humanist and historian, Mary's court poet and personal friend, but was critical of her reign in his later writings.

Knox's[215] chronicles, for if any of these infamous libels remain
while your days, use the law upon the keepers thereof, for
in that point I would have you a Pythagorean, to thing that
the spirits of these archi-bellowces[216] of rebellion, are flitted
into them that hoard their books, or maintain their opinions,
punishing them even as it were their authors risen again. But
by reading authentic histories and chronicles, you shall learn
experience by theoricke,[217] applying the bypast things to the
present estate, *quia nihil nunc dici aut sieri potest, quad non
dictum* and *factum sit prius;*[218] such is the continual volubility
of things earthly, according to the roundness of the world, and
volubility of the heavenly circles, which is expressed by the
wheels in Ezekiel's vision,[219] and counterfeited by the poets in
rota Fortunae.[220] And likewise by the knowledge of histories,
you shall know how to behave yourself to all ambassadors and
strangers, being able to discourse with them upon the estate
of their own country. As for the study of other liberal arts and
sciences, I would have you reasonably versed into them, but
not preassing to be a passe-master[221] in any of them; for that
can not but distract you from the points of your calling (as
I showed before) and when (by the enemy winning the town)
you shall be interrupted in your demonstration (as Archimedes

---

[215] **Knox** John Knox (c.1505–1572), protestant cleric who was in frequent
conflict with the Roman Catholic Mary.
[216] **archi-bellowces** large bellows (because they blow up the fires of rebellion)
[217] **theoricke** theory
[218] **quia...prius** *because nothing is said now that hasn't been said before* and
done before
[219] Ezek 1:15–21
[220] **rota Fortunae** *wheel of fortune.* As in "What goes around comes
around."
[221] **passe-master** a craftsman who has passed the examination for master's rank

was)[222] your people (I trow)[223] will look very bluntly upon it. I grant it is meet you have some entrance, specially in the mathematics, for the knowledge of the art military, in situation of camps, making fortifications, breaches or such like; and let not this your knowledge be dead without fruits (as Saint James speaks of faith)[224] but let it appear in your daily conversation, and in all the actions of your life.

Embrace true magnanimity, not in being vindictive, which the corrupted judgments of the world thinks to be true magnanimity, but by the contrary, in thinking your offender not worthy of your wrath, empyring[225] over your own passion, and triumphing in the commanding yourself to forgive, stewarding the effects of your courage and wrath, to be rightly employed upon repelling of injuries within, by revenge taking upon the oppressors and in revenging injuries without by just wars upon foreign enemies: and so, where you find a notable injury, spare not to give course to the torrents of your wrath; the wrath of a king is like to the roaring of a lion.[226]

Foster true humility in banishing pride, not only towards God (considering you differ not in stuff but in use and that only by his ordinance from the basest of your people) but also towards your parents.

And because it is likely by the course of nature, that my wife shall outlive me: as ever you think to purchase my blessing, honor your mother; set Bathsheba[227] in a throne on your

---

[222]"Marcellus" in Plutarch, *Lives of the Nobel Grecians and Romans.* Archimedes was said to have been cut down when he was so involved in a geometry problem that he ignored the orders of a Roman soldier during the conquest of Syracuse. Given the trouble that the Roman soldiery had just been suffering from his war machines, however, one suspects they might have been carrying a grudge.
[223]**trow** believe
[224]Jas 2:17 "Even so the faith, if it have no workes, is dead in it self."
[225]**empyring** governing, umpiring
[226]Prov 19:12
[227]Bathsheba was the mother of King Solomon, but perhaps James should have chosen a more auspicious example since, according to

right hand. Offend her for nothing, much less wrong her. Remember her

quae longa decem tulerit fastidia menses.[228]

And that your flesh and blood is made of hers, and begin not (like the young lords and lairds)[229] your first wars upon your mother, but preasse ever earnestly to deserve her blessing. Neither deceive yourself with many that say they care not for their parents curse so they deserve it not. Oh invert not the order of nature by judging you superiors, chiefly in your own particular! But assure yourself, the blessing or curse of the parents hath almost ever a prophetic power joined with it, and if there were no more, honor your parents for the lengthening of your own days (as God in his law promises.) honor also them that are *in loco parentum*[230] unto you, such as your governors and upbringers, and your preceptors; be thankful unto them and reward them, which is your duty and honor, but on the other part, let not this true humility stay your high indignation to appear when any great oppressors shall presume to come in your presence. Then frown as you ought; and in case they use a color of law in oppressing their poor ones (as over-many do) that which you can not mend by law, mend by the with drawing of your countenance from them: and once in the year cross them when their turns come athwart you, oppressing the oppressor according to Christ's parable of the two debtors.[231]

Keep true constancy, not only in your kindness towards honest men, but being also *invicti animi*[232] against all ad-

---

1Kings, she conspired with the cleric Nathan to deceive King David and advance Solomon over his older half-brother, the rightful heir.

[228]**quae...menses** *who fastidiously carried you for ten long months.*

[229]**lords and lairds** members of the peerage and the gentry, respectively. In this period a Scots laird was roughly equivalent to an English squire in the social hierarchy.

[230]**in loco parentum** *in the place of a parent.* Legal term.

[231] Mt 18:23–34

[232]**invicti animi** *[an] invincible spirit*

versities, not with that stoic insensible stupidity that proud inconstant Lipsius persuaded his Constantia.[233] But although you are not a stoic, not to feel calamities, yet let not the feeling of them so overrule and doazen[234] your reason, as may stay you from taking and using the best resolution for remedy that can be found out.

Use true liberality in rewarding the good, and bestowing frankly for your honor and weal; but provide how to have and cast not away without cause; and specially, enrich not yourself with extractions upon your subjects; but think the riches of your people your best pose, by the sins of the offenders making your kitchen to reik,[235] and in case necessity of wars or other extraordinaries compel you to lift subsidies, do it as rarely as you can, employing it only to the use it was ordained for, using yourself in that case as, *fidus depositarius*[236] to your people.

And principally exercise true wisdom, in discerning wisely betwixt true and false reports; first considering the nature of the person reporter; next, what interest he can have in the weal or evil of him whom of he makes the report; thirdly, the likelyhood of the purpose itself; and last the nature and bypast life of the dilated person.[237] And where you find a tratler,[238] away with him: and although it be true, that a prince can never without secrecy do great things, yet it is better ofttimes to try reports, than by credulity to foster suspicion up on an honest man; for since suspicion is the tyrant's sickness, as the fruits of an evil conscience, *potius in alterem partem peccato*,[239] I mean, in not mistrusting one whomto no such unhonesty was known

---

[233]Justus Lipsius (1547–1606) Belgian humanist whose book *De Constantia* (1584) was the seminal work of Neo-Stoicism. Lipsius lived in several countries, outwardly adopting the established religion in each, hence James' characterization of him as "inconstant."

[234]**doazen** benumb, stupefy

[235]**reik** smoke

[236]**fidus depositarius** *faithful trustee*

[237]**dilated person** the person reported on

[238]**tratler** tattler, prattler

[239]**potius. . . peccato** *better to make an error somewhere else*

before. But as for people that have slipped before, *argumen-tum a simili*[240] may justly breed prevention by foresight.

And to conclude my advice anent your behavior in your person: consider that God is the author of all virtue, having imprinted in men's minds by the very light of Nature, the love of all moral virtues, (as was seen by the virtuous lives of the old Romans). And preasse then to shine as far before your people in all virtue and honesty, as in greatness of rank, that the use thereof in all your actions, may turn (with time) in a natural habitude unto you, that as by their hearing of your laws, so by their sight of your person, both their eyes and their ears, may lead and allure them to love of virtue and hatred of vice.

---

[240]**argumentum a simili** *[an] argument from similitude*

Book III: Anent a King's Behavior in Indifferent Things

It is a true old saying, that a king is as one set on a scaffold, whose smallest actions and gestures all the people gazingly[241] do behold: and therefore although a king be never so precise in the discharging of his office, the people who see but the outward part, will ever judge of the substance by the circumstances, and according to the outward appearance (if his behavior be light or dissolute) will conceive preoccupied conceits of the king's inward intention, which although with time (the trier of all truth) it will vanish, by the evidence of the contrary events, yet *interim patitur justus*[242] and the prejudged conceits will (in the meantime) breed contempt, the mother of rebellion and disorder; and besides that it is certain, that all the indifferent actions and behavior of a man, have a certain holding and dependence, either upon virtue or vice, according as they are used or ruled, for there is not a middes[243] betwixt them, no more nor betwixt their rewards, Heaven and Hell.

Be careful then (my son) so to frame all your indifferent actions and outward behavior, as they may serve for the furtherance and forth-setting of your virtuous qualities.

---

[241]**gazingly** intently
[242]**interim patitur justus** *justifiably suffer in the meantime*
[243]**middes** middle or average

BASILIKON DORON

The whole indifferent actions of a man, I divide into two sorts: in his behavior in things necessary, as food, sleeping, raiment, speaking, writing, and gesture, and in things not necessary (though convenient and lawful) as pastimes or exercises, and using of company for recreation.

As to the indifferent things necessary, although that of themselves they cannot be wanted, and so in that case are not indifferent, as likewise in case they be not used with moderation on declining so to the extremity which is vice—yet the quality and form of using them, may smell of virtue or of vice, and be great furtherers to any of them.

To begin first then at the things necessary, one of the publicest indifferent actions of a king, and that manyest[244] (especially strangers) will narrowly take heed to, is his manner of refection at his table and his behavior thereat. Therefore, as king's use oft to eat publicly, it is meet and honorable that you also do so, as well to eschew the opinion that you love not to haunt[245] company, which is one of the marks of a tyrant: as likewise, that your delight to eat privately, be not thought to be for private satisfying of your gluttony, which you would be ashamed should be publicly seen. Let your table be honorable served, but serve your appetite with few dishes (as young Cyrus did)[246] which both is wholesomest and freest from the vice of delicacy, which is a degree of gluttony: and use most to eat of reasonable rude and common meats, as well for making your body strong and durable for travel, as that you may be the hartlier received by your mean subjects in their houses, when their cheer may suffice you; which otherwise would be imputed to you for pride, and breed disdain in them. Let all your food be of simplest, without composition or sauces, which are more like medicines than meat: the using of them was counted among the ancient Romans, a filthy vice of delicacy

---

[244]**manyest** majority
[245]**haunt** frequent; stay near
[246]Xenophon, *Cyropaedia*, I:3:4

(because they serve only for pleasing of the taste, and not for satisfying of the appetite) abhorring Aptius their own citizen, for his vice of delicacy. Like as both the Greeks and Romans had in detestation the very name of Philoxenus, for his filthy wish of the cranne-craige.[247] And therefore was that sentence used among them against their artificial false appetites: *Optimum condimentum fames*[248] But beware with using excess of meat and drink; and chiefly beware of drunkenness, which is a beastly vice, namely in a king. But specially beware with it because it is one of those vices that increases with age. In the form of your meat eating, be neither uncivil (like a gross Cynic) nor affectedly mignarde[249] (like a dainty dame) but eat in a manly, round, and honest fashion. It is nowise comely to dispatch affairs, or to be pensive at meat: but keep than an open and cheerful countenance, garring them read pleasant histories unto you, that profit may be mixed with pleasure. And when you are evil disposed, entertain pleasant, quick but honest discourses.

And because meat provokes sleeping, be also moderate in your sleep, for it goes much by use; and remember, that if your whole life were divided in four parts, three of them would be found to be consumed on meat, drink, and sleep. But albeit ordinary times would commonly be kept in meat and sleep; yet use yourself whiles so, that any time in the four and twenty hours may be alike to you for any of them, that thereby your diet may be accommodate to your affairs, and not your affairs to your diet—not therefore using yourself to over great softness

---

[247] **cranne-craige** crane's neck. Philoxenus was a notable gormandizer, even by Roman standards, and once wished for a neck as long as a crane's so he could savor the sensation of eating all the more. It is unlikely that his fellows detested him for this, however, as much as for his trick of deliberately sneezing on the food so no one else could eat it. "Whether 'Live Unknown' be a Wise Precept" in Plutarch, *Moralia*. q.v. Rabelais' *Gargantua and Pantagruel* 5:XLII.

[248] **Optimum condimentum fames.** *Hunger is the best seasoning.*

[249] **mignarde** delicate; effeminate

and delicacy in your sleep more nor in your meat, and specially in case you have ado with the wars.

Let not your chamber be throng and common the time of your rest as well for comeliness, as for eschewing of carrying clatters out of the same. Let them that have the credit to serve in your chamber be trusty and secret—for a king will have need to use secrecy in many things—but yet behave yourself so in your greatest secrets, as you need no be ashamed suppose they were all proclaimed at the cross. But specially see that those of your chamber be of a sound fame, and without blemish. Take no heed to any of your dreams; for all prophecies, visions, and prophetic dreams are accomplished and ceased in Christ: and therefore take no heed to freats[250] either in dreams or any other things, for that error proceeds of ignorance and is unworthy of a Christian, who should be assured *quad omnia sunt sancta sanctis*,[251] all days and meats being alike to Christians (as Paul says).[252]

Next follows to speak of raiment, the on-putting whereof is the ordinary action that follows next to sleep. Be also moderate in your raiment; neither over-superfluous (like a debouched waster) nor yet over-base (like a miserable peddler) not artificially trimmed and decked (like a courtesan:) nor yet over sluggishly clothed (like a country clown) not over slightly (like a Candie soldier[253] or a vain young courtier) nor yet over gravely (like a minister) but in your garments be proper, cleanly, comely and honest; wearing your clothes in a careless yet comely form: keeping in them a middle form, *inter toga-*

---

[250]**freats** superstitious notions, premonitions
[251]**quad... sanctis** *that everything is confirmed [as] sacred*
[252]Rom 14:14 "I knowe, & am persuaded through the Lord Jesus, that there is nothing uncleane of it self: but unto him that judgeth anything to be uncleane, to him it is uncleane."
[253]**Candie soldier** a soldier of Candia (modern Heraklion) in Crete where the weather is much warmer than in Scotland, so that soldiers wear less clothing

tus[254] and *palliatus*,[255] betwixt the gravity of the one and the lightness of the other: thereby to signify, that by your calling you are mixed of both the professions, *togatus* as a judge making and pronouncing the law, *palliatus* by the power of the sword: as your office is likewise mixed betwixt the ecclesiastical and civil estate: for a king is not *mere laicus*,[256] as both the Papists and the Anabaptists would have him, to the which error also our Puritans incline over-far. But to return to the purpose of garments, they ought to be used according to their first institution by God, which was for three causes: to hide our nakedness and shame, and consequently to make us more comely, and thirdly, to preserve us from the injuries of heat and cold. If to hide our nakedness and shameful parts, these natural parts ordained to be hid, should not then be represented by any forms in the clothes, as the great filthy baloppes[257] do (bearing the pensel of Priapus)[258] which therefore I think the only unlawful form of clothes. And if they should help our comeliness, they should not then by their painted preined[259] fashion serve for baits to filthy lechery, as false hair and fairding[260] do among unchaste women. And if they should preserve us from the injuries of heat and cold, and although it be praiseworthy and necessary in a prince, to be *patiens algoris* and *aestus*,[261] when he shall have ado with wars upon the fields, yet I think it meeter that you go both clothed and armed, nor naked to the battle;[262] except you would make you light for

---

[254]**inter togatus** between wearing the toga i.e. a citizen, and thus eligible to hold public offices, such as magistracies

[255]**palliatus** wearing a Greek cloak, which was part of most ancient military uniforms, representing military authority

[256]**mere laicus** *mere layman*, i.e. not part of the clergy

[257]**baloppes** codpiece

[258]**pensel of Priapus** A *pensel* is a small streamer or flag. Priapus was a god of reproduction, commonly symbolized by a phallus.

[259]**preined** decked, trimmed

[260]**fairding** painting, disguising

[261]**patiens...aestus** *willing to endure chill* and *heat*

[262]James may have been thinking of the ancient Celtic custom of going

away-running; and yet for cowards, *metus addet alas.*[263] And shortly, in your clothes keep a proportion, as well with the seasons of the year, as of your age; in the fashions of them being careless, using them according to the common form of the time, whiles richlier, whiles meanlier clothed as occasion serves, without keeping any precise rule therein; for if your mind be found occupied upon them, it will be thought idle otherwise, as Caesar said *de compto juvene,*[264] whose spirit therefore be feared not; but specially eschew to be effeminate in your clothes, in the perfuming, preining, or suchlike: and fail never in time of wars to be galliardest[265] and bravest, both in clothes and countenance: and make not a fool of yourself in disguising or wearing long your hair or nails, which are but excrements of Nature, and betray such issuers of them, to be either of a vindictive, or a vain light natural. Especially, make no vows in such vain and outward things as concern either meat or clothes.

Let yourself and all your court wear no ordinary armor with your clothes, but such as is knightly and honorable; I mean rapier swords and daggers: for toilsome weapons in the court betoken confusion in the country:[266] and therefore banish not only from your court all traitorous offensive weapons forbidden by the laws, as guns and suchlike (whereof I spake already) but also such traitorous defensive arms, as secrets, plate-sleeves, and suchlike unseen armor: for (besides that the

---

into battle naked, but it scarcely seems likely that an early modern king tempted to do so.

[263] **metus addet alas** *fear increases [when] nourished*

[264] **de compto juvene** *from youthful embellishment*

[265] **galliardest** sprightly, brisk, lively

[266] The rapier, while very popular in the Elizabethan period, was comparatively new to the British Isles, having arrived some time in the 1570s. The "toilsome weapons" referred to here might have included any of a stunning variety of swords then in use, including the two-handed Scots claymore (which attained its longest length in this century), as well as polearms and impact weapons, none of which would have been appropriate for court wear.

wearers thereof may be presupposed to have a secret evil intention) they want both the uses that defensive armor is ordained
for; which is, to be able to hold our violence, and by their outward glancing in their enemies eyes, to strike a terror in their
hearts, where by the contrary they can serve for neither, being
not only unable to resist, but dangerous for shots, and giving
no outward glance against the enemy, being only ordained for
betraying under trust, whereof honest men should be ashamed
to bear the outward badge, not resembling the thing they are
not.[267] And of answer against their arguments, I know none
but the old Scots fashion, which if it be wrong, is no more to
be allowed for ancientness, nor the old messe is which also our
forebears used.

The next thing that you have to take heed to, is your speaking and language, whereunto I join your gesture, since action
is one of the chieftest qualities that is required in an orator,
for as the tongue speaks to the ears, so doth the gesture speak
to the eyes of the auditoure.[268] In both your speaking and
your gesture than, use a natural and plain form, not fairded
with artifice: for (as the Frenchmen say) *Rien countersaict
sin*[269] but eschew all affected forms in both. In your language
be plain, honest, natural, comely, clean, short, and senten-
tious; eschewing both the extremities, as well in not using
a rustic corrupt leid,[270] not yet book language and pen and
inkhorn terms: but let the greatest part of your eloquence
consist in a natural, clear, and sensible form of the delivery

---

[267]Full armor, by this period, had been discarded in favor of mobility
in active military service and was retained only for parades and com-
petitive jousting. The "ordinary amour" of which James writes might
have provided some minimal protection against the knives of assas-
sins, but may also have been worn as a fashion statement, to show that
the wearer was a "fighting man". In its most common form it would
have consisted of small metal plates sewn into a leather doublet or
jacket.
[268]**auditoure** audience
[269]**Rien...sin** *Nothing counteracts sin.*
[270]**leid** song, lay

of your mind, built aye upon certain and good grounds, tempering it with gravity, quickness or merriness according to the subject, and occasion of the time, not taunting in theology, nor alleging scripture in drinking purposes (as over many do) use also the like form in your gesture, neither looking silly (like a stupid pedant) nor unsettledly with an uncouth morgue[271] (like a new-come-over Cavalier) but let your behavior be natural, grave, and according to the fashion of your country. Be not over sparing in your courtesies, for that will be imputed to incivility and arrogancy; nor yet over prodigal in jowking[272] or nodding at every step, for that form of being popular, becomes better aspiring Absaloms[273] than lawful kings; framing ever your gesture according to your present actions, looking gravely and with a majesty when you sit in judgment, or give audience to ambassadors: homely, when you are in private with your own servants: merely, when you are at any pastime or merry discourse, and let your countenance smell of courage and magnanimity when you are at the wars: and remember (I say over again) to be plain and sensible in your language; for besides that it is the tongue's office to be the messenger of the mind, it may be thought a point of imbecility of the spirit in a king to speak obscurely, much more untruly, as if he stood awe of any in uttering his thoughts; except some unhappy mutiny or sudden rebellion were blazed up: then indeed it is a lawful policy, to bear with that present fiery confusion by fair general speeches, (keeping you as far as you can from direct promises) while the fire be quenched, and that confused mass separated; and to do otherwise, it were no magnanimity, but rash tempting of God. Remember also, to put a difference betwixt your

---

[271]**morgue** a strange, solemn face
[272]**jowking** bending down the body with a quick motion
[273]**Absalom** The third son of King David. He conspired to kill his half-brother Amnon in vengeance for Amnon's rape of Absalom's sister Tamar. Later, he led a bloody but ultimately unsuccessful insurrection against David. See 2Sam 3–19 The story also appears in Josephus' *Antiquities of the Jews* VII:8–10.

form of language in reasoning, and your pronouncing of sentences or declarator[274] of your will in judgment, or any other wise in the points of your office: for in the former case, you must reason pleasantly and patiently, not like a king, but like a private man and a scholar: otherwise, your impatience of contradiction will be interpreted to be for lack of reason on your part; where in the points of your office, you should ripely advise[275] indeed before you give forth your sentence, but fra[276] it be given forth, the suffering of any contradiction, diminishes the majesty of your authority and makes the process endless; the like form should also be observed by all your inferior judges and magistrates.

Now as to your writing, which is nothing else, but a form of enregistrate[277] speech; use a plain, short, but stately style, both in your proclamations and missives, especially to foreign princes: and if your engine[278] spur you to write any works either in verse or in prose, I cannot but allow you to practice it, but take no longsome works in hand for distracting you from your calling. Flatter not yourself in your labors, but before they be set forth, let them first be privily censured by some of the best skilled men in that craft, that in these works you mell with. And because your writs will remain as true pictures of your mind to all posterities, let them be free of all uncomeliness and unhonesty: and according to Horace's counsel *de arte poetica,*

Nonum premantur in annum.[279]

---

[274]**declarator** a formal judicial declaration of a particular fact or legal right
[275]**ripely advise** give sufficient consideration
[276]**fra** from the time
[277]**enregistrate** recorded
[278]**engine** genius, wit, disposition
[279]**Nonum... annum** *keep it back nine years.* The full quote is "Weigh your work well, and keep it back nine years."

I mean both your verse and your prose: letting first that fury and heat cool at leisure wherewith they were written, and then as an uncouth judge and censure, revising them over again, *antequam ultimam adhibeas manum.*[280] If you would write worthily, choose subjects worthy of you, that be not full of vanity, and delighting ever to be plain and sensible: and if you write in verse, remember that it is not the principal part of a poem to rhyme right, and flow well with many pretty words; but the chief commendation of a poem, is, that when the verse shall be shaken sundry in prose, it shall be found so rich in quick inventions and poetic floures[281] as it shall retain the luster of a poem although in prose: and I would also advise you to write in your language: *antequam ultimam adhibeas manum* for there is nothing left to be said in Greek and Latin already,[282] and enough of poor scholars would match you in these languages: and besides that, it best becomes a king to purify and make famous his own language, wherein he may go before all his subjects; as it sets him well to do in all honest and lawful things.

And among all unnecessary things that are lawful and expedient, I think exercises of the body most commendable to be used by a young prince, in such honest games or pastimes as may further habilitie[283] and maintain health: for albeit I grant it be most requisite for a king to exercise his engine (which surely with idleness will rust and become blunt) yet certainly bodily exercises and games are very commendable, as well for banishing of idleness (the mother of all vices) as for making his body able and durable for travel, which is very necessary for a king. But from this count I debar all rum-

---

[280]**antequam...manum** *Until applying the final touch.* Likely a paraphrase of Horace's. *Ars Poetica* 292–294.

[281]**floures,** decorations, flourishes (lit. *flowers*)

[282]While it is hard to fault the advice for a king to write in the common language, Latin remained an important language for scholarly works for at least another century.

[283]**habilitie** ability; physical strength

ling[284] violent exercises; as the football,[285] meeter for laming nor making able the users thereof: as likewise such tumbling tricks as only serve for comedians and gysares[286] to win their bread with. But the exercises that I would have you to use (although but moderately, not making a craft of them) are running, leaping, wrestling, fencing, dancing, and playing at the caitche.[287] And the honorablest and most commendable games that you can use are games on horseback; for it becomes a prince best of any man to be a fair and good horseman. Use therefore to ride and dantone great and courageous horses, that I may say of you (as Phillip said of great Alexander his son) Μαχεδονια΄ ὄ σε χωρει;[288] and use specially such games on horseback as may teach you to handle your arms thereon, such as the tilt, the ring, and low riding for handling of your sword.[289]

I can not omit here the hunting, specially with running hounds, which is the most honorable and noblest sort thereof, for it is a thievish form of hunting to shoot with guns and bows, and greyhound hunting is not so martial nor noble a game. But because I would be thought a partial praiser of the this sport, I remit you to Xenophon, an old and famous writer, who had no mind of flattering either me or you in this purpose, and who also sets down a fair pattern for the education of a young

---

[284]**rumling** noisy, rambunctious

[285]The various forms of football have a very long history in the British Isles. Until their adoption by public schools in the Victorian period, they were generally considered to be peasant games.

[286]**gysares** maskers or harlequins, but they would be more likely to have been locals dressing for a holiday celebration than professionals seeking to "win their bread"

[287]**caitche** a type of handball game that was popular in James' Scottish court

[288]*A Macedonian in [his natural] place.*

[289]All three of these were exercises involving attacking a stationary target from a moving horse. The tilt was a pivoting dummy for jousting practice and the ring was meant to speared on the tip of the lance.

king, under the supposed name of Cyrus.[290] As for hawking I condemn it not, but I must praise it more sparingly, because it neither resembles the wars so near as hunting doth in making a man hardy and skillful riding in all grounds: and is more uncertain and subject to mischances; and (which is worst of all) is therethrough[291] an extreme stirrer up of passions: but in using either of these games observe that moderation, that you slip not therewith with the hours appointed for your affairs which you ought ever precisely for to keep, remembering that these games are but ordained for you, in enabling you for your office for which you are ordained.

And as sitting house pastimes, (wherewith men by driving time spur a free and fast enough horse, as the proverb is) although they are not profitable for the exercise either of mind or body, yet I cannot utterly condemn them, since they may whiles supply the room, which being tome[292] would be patent to pernicious idleness, *quia nihil potest esse vacuum.*[293] I will not therefore agree with the curiosity of Danaeus in his book *De Lusu Aleae*[294] and most of the French ministers (although otherwise surely I reverence them as notable and godly men) for they are deceived therein, in founding their argument upon a mistaken ground, which is, that the playing at cards or dice is a kind of casting of lot, and therefore unlawful: wherein they deceive themselves for the casting of lot was used for trial of the truth in any obscure thing that otherwise could not be gotten cleared, and therefore was a sort of prophecy, where by the contrary, no man goes to any of these plays to

---

[290]Xenophon *Cyropaedia,* I:2:10
[291]**therethrough** thereby
[292]**tome** drawn out
[293]**quia…vacuum** *because nothing can be empty/idle* This is probably a wordplay on Cicero's *The Nature of the Gods* (Book I, XXIII): Cicero is referring to a physical vacuum but the word also means "idle" in Latin.
[294]**De Lusu Aleae** *About Playing Gambling Games.* Lambert Danaeus was also known for writing about witchcraft, another of James' interests.

clear any obscure truth, but only to gage[295] so much of his own money as he pleases, upon the hazard of the running of the cards or dice, as well as he would do upon the speed of a horse or a dog, or any such like gaygeour,[296] and so if they be unlawful, all gaygeours upon uncertainties must likewise be condemned; not that thereby I take the defense of vain carders and dicers that waste their moyen,[297] and their time (whereof few consider the preciousness) upon prodigal and continual playing, no I would rather allow it to be discharged where such corruptions cannot be eschewed, but only I cannot condemn you at some times when you have no other thing ado[298] (as a good king will be seldom) and are weary of reading or evil disposed in your person, then (I say) may you lawfully play at the cards or tables: for as to dicing, I think it becomes best debouched soldiers to play at on the head of their drums, being only ruled by hazard, and subject to knavish cogging.[299] And as for the chess, I think is over fonde,[300] because it is over-wise and philosophic a folly; for where all such light plays are ordained to free men's heads for a time, from the faschious[301] thoughts on their affairs, it by the contrary fills and troubles men's heads with as many faschious toyes[302] of the play, as before it was filled with thoughts on his affairs.

But in your playing I would have you to keep three rules, first or[303] you play, consider you do it only for your recreation, and resolve to hazard the loss of all that you play: and next, for

---

[295] **gage** to pledge or wager

[296] **gaygeour** a wager

[297] **moyen** property, means

[298] **ado** going on; afoot

[299] **cogging** drinking. A cog was a small wooden bowl or cup used to hold liquor.

[300] **fonde** silly, stupid, unprofitable

[301] **faschious** troublesome

[302] **toyes** toys. i.e. the player will be preoccupied toying with chess problems

[303] **or** ere, before

that cause play no more nor you care to cast among pages,[304] and last, play always fair play precisely, that you come not in use of tricking and lying in mowes: otherwise (if you cannot keep these rules) my counsel is that you utterly abstain from these plays: for neither a mad passion for loss, not falsehood used to gain with, can be called any play.

Now, it is not only lawful but necessary, that you have company meet for every thing you take on hand, as well in your games and exercises as in your grave and earnest affairs, but learn to distinguish time according to the occasion, choosing your company accordingly. Confer not with hunters at your counsel nor in your counsel affairs; nor dispatch not affairs at hunting or other games: and have the like respect to the seasons of your age, using your sorts of recreation and company therefore agreeing thereunto: for it becomes best (as kindliest) every age to smell of the own quality (insolence and unlawful things being always eschewed) and that a colt should draw the plow and an old horse run away with the harrows. But take heed specially, that your company for recreation be chosen of honest persons not defamed or vicious, mixing filthy talk with merriness. *Corrumpunt bonos mores colloquia prava.*[305] But specially abstain from haunting before your marriage the idle company of dames, which are nothing else but *alliciamenta veneris.*[306] And abuse not yourself in making your sporters[307] your counselors. Specially delight not to keep ordinarily in your company, comedians, or balladines,[308] for the tyrants delighted most in them, and delighted to make comedies and tragedies themselves.[309] Whereupon the answer that a philoso-

---

[304]**no more ... pages** no more than you would tip servants. i.e. Only play for pocket money.
[305]**Corrumpunt...prava** *Evil conversation will corrupt good morals.* Erasmus, after 1 Cor. 33
[306]**alliciamenta veneris** *alluring Venuses*
[307]**sporters** companions in leisure activities
[308]**balladines** dancers
[309]Once he ascended to the English throne James became an important

pher gave one of them thereanents, is now come in a proverb, *Reduc me latomias:*[310] and all the ruse that Nero made of himself when he died was *Hodie moritur optimus tragaeda,*[311] as indeed his whole life was all but one tragedy.

Delight not also to be in your own person a player upon instruments, especially on such as commonly men win their living with, nor yet to be fine of any mechanic craft: Du Bartas[312] says, *Leur esprit s'en suit au bout des doigts.*[313] But spare not whiles by merry company to be free from importunity: for you should be moved with reason (which is the only quality whereby men differ from beasts) and not with importunity for the which cause (as also for augmenting your majesty) you shall not be so facile of access giving at all times as I have been: and yet not altogether retired or locked up like the kings of Persia, appointing also certain hours for public audience.

And since my trust is, that God hath ordained you for more kingdoms nor this, (as I have oft already said) preasse by the outward behavior as well of your own person as of your court in all indifferent things, to allure piece and piece the rest of your kingdoms to follow the fashions of that kingdom of yours that you find most civil, easiest to be ruled, and most

---

patron of the theater, so apparently it is permissible to sponsor comedies and tragedies as long as the King is not involved in the production itself.

[310] **Reduc que latomias.** *Put me back in the quarries.* Reputed words of Philoxenus of Cythera on being delivered from a quarry work gang to give his opinion of Dionysus I's poetry. Reported in both Plutarch's *Moralia* ("On the Fortune of Alexander") and Diodorus Siculus' *Library of History* (Book XV, Chapter 6).

[311] **Hodie...tragaeda** *Today dies a great tragedian!* But according to both Suetonius (*The Lives of the Twelve Caesars* 6:49) and Dio (62) Nero's actual last words were *Quales artifex pereo!*"What an artist perishes in me!"

[312] Du Bartas, Gillaume de Saluste (1544–1590). Poet and courtier to Henri de Navarre. James was an avid admirer and, at one point, contributed a translation of one of his poems for a Scots anthology of Du Bartas' works.

[313] **Leur... doigts** *Their minds follow at your fingertips*

obedient to the laws—for outward and indifferent things are ever the shadows and allurers to virtue or vice—but beware of thrawing or constraining them thereto, letting it be brought on with time and at leisure, specially by mixing through ally and daily conversation, the men of every kingdom with another, as may with time make them to grow and weld all in one: which may easily be done in this Isle of Britain, being all but one isle, and allready joined in unity of religion and language.

And for conclusion of this my whole treatise, remember (my son) by your true and constant depending upon God, to procure a blessing to all your actions in your office, by outward using of your office to testify to inward uprightness of your heart, and by things to set forth the true shadow of your virtuous disposition. And in respect of the greatness and weight of your burden, to be patient in hearing, keeping your heart free from preoccupation, cold in deliberation, ripe in concluding, and constant in your resolution: for better it is to bide at your resolution, although there were some wrong in it, than by daily changing to effectuate nothing; taking the pattern thereof from the microcosm of your own body: wherein you have two eyes, signifying great foresight and providence, with a narrow looking in all things: and also two ears, signifying patient hearing, and that of both the parties: but he have but one tongue, for pronouncing a plain, sensible, and uniform sentence, and but one head, and one heart, for keeping a constant and uniform resolution according to your apprehension; having two hands, with many fingers for quick execution, in employing all instruments meete for effectuating your deliberations.

But forget not to digest ever your passion before you determine upon anything, since *Ira furor brevis est*[314] uttering only your anger according to the Apostle's rule,[315] *Irascimini sed*

---

[314]**Ira... est;** *Anger is [a] brief insanity.* traditional legal maxim
[315]Eph 4:26 "Be angry, but sinne not: let not the sunne go downe upon your wrath"

ne peccetis,[316] taking pleasure not only to reward but advance the good (which is a chief point of a king's glory) but make none over-great, but according as the power of the country may bear; and punishing the evil, but every man according to his own offense; not punishing nor blaming the father of the son, not the brother for the brother: much less generally to hate a whole race, *nam omnia delicta sunt personalia.*[317]

And above all, let the measure of your love to everyone be according to the measure of his virtue, letting your favor be no longer bound to any, than the continuance of his virtuous disposition shall deserve: not admitting the excuse upon a just revenge, to procure oversight to an injury for the first injury is committed against the party: but the parties revenging thereof at his own hand, is a wrong committed against you, in usurping your office whomto only the sword belongs for revenging of all the injuries committed against any of your people.

Thus hoping in the goodness of God, that your natural inclination shall have a happy sympathy with these precepts, making the wise man's schoolmaster (which is the example of others) to be your teacher, according to that old verse,

Faelix, quem faciunt aliena pericula cautum[318]

Eschewing so the over-late repentance by your own experience (which is the schoolmaster of fools) I will for end of all, require you (my son) as ever you think to deserve my fatherly blessing, to keep continually before the eyes of your mind, the greatness of your charge, making the faithful and due discharge thereof the principal butt you shoot at in all your actions, counting it ever the principal; and all your other actions but as accessories to be employed as middeses for the

---

[316]Ps 4:5 "Be ye angry, and sin not: the things you say in your hearts, be sorry for them upon your beds."

[317]**nam … personalia** *For in fact all trespasses are personal.* Legal maxim.

[318]**Faelix…cautum** *Happy is the man who can learn from the dangers of others.* Proverbial, originally from *Aesop's Fables.*

furthering of that principle, and being content to let others excel in other things. Let it be your chiefest earthly glory, to excel in your own craft: according to that worthy sentence of that sublime and heroic poet Virgil, wherein also my dictone[319] is included:

Excudent alii spirantia mollius aera,
Credo equidem: vivos ducent de marmore voltus
Orabunt causas melius; caelique meatus
Describent radio, et surgentia sidera dicent.
Tu, regere imperio populos, Romane, memento:
Hae tibi erunt artes; pacisque imponere morem.
PARCERE SUBJECTIS, ET DEBELLARE
    SUPERBOS.[320]

---

[319]**dictone** dictum

[320]Others will forge breathing bronzes more smoothly
    I believe, and draw forth living features from marble.
    They will plead lawsuits better and trace the movements
    Of the sky with a rod and describe the rising stars.
    You, Roman, govern the nations with your power- remember:
    These will be your arts—to impose the ways of peace,
    TO SHOW MERCY TO THE CONQUERED AND SUBDUE THE
        PROUD.
    Virgil, *Aeneid*, Bk. VI Lines 847–853

To the Reader

Charitable Reader, it is one of the golden sentences, which Christ our savior uttered to his apostles, that there is nothing so covered, that shall not be revealed, neither so hid, that shall not be known: and whatsoever they have spoken in darkness, should be heard in the light: and that which they have spoken in darkness, should not be heard in the light: and that which they had spoken in the ear in secret place, should be publicly preached on the tops of the houses.[321] And since he hath said it, most true must it be, since the author thereof is the fountain and very being of truth, which should move all godly and honest men, to be very wary in all their secretest actions, and whatsoever middeses they use for attaining to their most wished ends: least otherwise how avowable soever the mark be, whereat they aim, the middeses being discovered to be shameful, whereby they climb; it may turn to the disgrace both of the good work itself, and of the author thereof: since the deepest of our secrets, can not be hid from that all-seeing eye, and penetrant light, piercing through the bowels of very darkness itself.

But as this is generally true in the actions of all men, so is it more specially true in the affairs of kings. For kings being public persons, by reason of their office and authority, are as it were set (as it was said of old) upon a public stage, in the sight of all the people; where all the beholders eyes are attentively bent, to look and pry in the least circumstance

---

[321]Lk 12:2–3

of their secretest drifts, which should make kings the more careful, not to harbor the secretest thought in their mind, but such as in the own time they shall not be ashamed openly to avouch: assuring themselves that Time, the mother of Verity, will in the due season bring her own daughter to perfection.

The true practice hereof, I have as a king oft found in my own person; though I thank God, never to my shame: having laid my account, ever to walk as in the eyes of the Almighty; examining ever so the secretest of my drifts, before I gave them course, as how they might some day bide the touchstone of a public trial. And amongst the rest of my secret actions, which have (unlooked for of me) come to public knowledge, it hath so fared with my $Βασιλικου$ $δωρον$,[322] directed to my eldest son; which I wrote for exercise of my own engine, and instruction of him, who is appointed by God (I hope) to sit on my throne after me. For the purpose and matter thereof being only fit for a king, as teaching him his office; and the person whomfor it was ordained, a king's heir, whose secret counselor and faithful admonisher it must be; I thought it no wise convenient, nor comely, that either it should to all be proclaimed, which to one only appertained (and specially being a messenger betwixt two conjunct persons) or yet that the mold, whereupon he should frame his future behavior, when he comes both unto the perfection of his years; and possession of his inheritance, should before the hand, be made common to the people, the subject of his future happy government. And therefore for the more secret, and close-keeping of them, I only permitted seven of them to be printed; the printer being first sworn for secrecy: and these seven I dispersed amongst some of my trustiest servants, to be kept closely by them: least in case by the iniquity, or wearing of time, any of them might have been lost, yet some of them might have remained after me, as witnesses to my son, both of the honest integrity of my heart, and of my fatherly affection and natural care toward him. But since contrary to my

---

[322] $Βασιλικου$ $δωρον$ Basilikon Doron

intention and expectation, as I have already said, this book is now vented, and set forth to the public view of the world, and consequently subject to every man's censure, as the current of his affection leads him; I am now forced, as well for resisting to the malice of the children of envy, who like wasps, suck venom out of every wholesome herb; as for the satisfaction of the godly honest sort, in anything that they may mistake therein; both to publish and spread the true copies thereof; for defacing of the false copies that are already spread, as I am informed: as likewise, by this preface, to clear such parts thereof, as in respect of the concise shortness of my style, may be misinterpreted therein.

To come then particularly to the matter of my book, there are two special great points; which (as I am informed) the malicious sort of men have detracted therein; and some of the honest sort have seemed a little to mistake: whereof the first and greatest is, that some sentences therein should seem to furnish grounds to men to doubt of my sincerity in that religion, which I have ever constantly professed: the other is, that in some parts thereof, I should seem to nourish in my mind, a vindictive resolution against England, or at the least, some principals there, for the queen my mother's quarrel.

The first calumny (most grievous indeed) is grounded upon the sharp and bitter words, that therein are used in the description of the humors of Puritans, and rash-heady preachers, that think it their honor to contend with kings and perturb whole kingdoms. The other point is only grounded upon the straight charge I give my son, not to hear, nor suffer any unreverent speeches or books against any of his parents or progenitors: wherein I do allege my own experience anent the queen my mother: affirming that I never found any, that were of perfite age the time of her reign here, so steadfastly true to me in all my troubles, as these that constantly kept their allegiance to her in her time. But if the charitable reader will advisedly consider, both the method and matter of my treatise, he will easily judge, what wrong I have sustained by the carping at both. For my book, suppose very small, being divided in three several parts; the first part thereof only treats of a king's duty towards God in religion: wherein I have so clearly made profession of my religion, calling it the religion wherein I was brought up, and ever made profession of, and wishing him ever to continue in the same, as the only true form of God's worship that I would have thought my sincere plainness in that first part upon that subject, should have dited the mouth of the most envious *Momus*,[323] that ever Hell did hatch, from the barking at any other part of my book upon that ground; except they would allege me to be contrary to myself, which in so small a volume would smell of too great weakness, and slipperiness of memory. And the second part of my book, teaches my son how to use his office, in the administration of justice, and politic government: the third only containing a king's outward behavior in these things, and the virtuous qualities of his mind: and how they should serve for truchmen[324] to interpret the inward disposition of the mind, to the eyes of them that cannot see farther within him, and therefore must only judge of him by the outward appearance. So as if there were no more to be looked into, but the very method and order of the book, it will sufficiently clear me of that first and grievousest imputation, in the point of religion: since in the first part, where religion is only treated of, I speak so plainly. And what in other parts I speak of Puritans, it is only one of their moral faults, in that part where I speak of policy: declaring when they condemn the law and sovereign authority, what exemplar punishment they deserve for the same. And now as to the matter itself whereupon this scandal is taken, that I may sufficiently satisfy all honest men, and by a just apology raise up a brazen wall or bulwark against all the darts of the envious, I will the more narrowly ripe up the words, whereat they seem to be somewhat stomached.

---

[323]**Momus** the Greek god of mockery and satire.
[324]**truchmen** interpreters, translators

TO THE READER

First than, as to the name of Puritans, I am not ignorant that the style thereof doth properly belong only to that vile sect amongst the Anabaptists, called the Family of Love[325] because they think themselves only pure, and in a manner without sin, the only true church, and only worthy to be participant of the sacraments; and all the rest of the world to be but abomination in the sight of God. Of this special sect I principally mean, when I speak of Puritans; diverse of them, as Browne[326], Penry,[327] and others, having at sundry times come in Scotland, to sow their people amongst us (and from my heart I wish, that they had left no scholars behind them, who by their fruits will in the own time be manifested) and partly, indeed, I give this style to such brain-sick and heady preachers, their disciples and followers, as refusing to be called of that sect, yet participates too much with their humors, in maintaining the above mentioned errors; not only agreeing with the general rule of all Anabaptists, in the contempt of the civil magistrate, and in leaning to their own dreams and revelations; but particularly with this sect, in accounting all men profane that swear not to all their fantasies; in making for every particular question of the policy of the church, as great commotion, as if the article of the trinity were called in controversy; in making the scriptures to be ruled by their conscience, and not their conscience by the scripture; and he that denies the least iota of their grounds, *sit tibi tanquam ethnicus*

---

[325]**Family of Love** a sect of pacifist nonconformist protestants which flourished throughout Northern Europe from the 16th through 18th centuries. It is generally agreed that James' criticism applied to Puritans in general, but that he adopted the Family of Love as a scapegoat because he was trying to placate more powerful Protestant factions at the time of the book's rerelease.

[326]Robert Browne (1550s-1633). The leader of a separatist movement from the Church of England. Many of the early settlers in New England were Brownists.

[327]John Penry (1559–1593) Welsh Puritan preacher, pamphleteer, and martyr.

et publicanus;[328] not worthy to enjoy the benefit of breathing, much less to participate with them of the sacraments: and before that any of their grounds be impugned, let king, people, law and all be tread underfoot. Such holy wars are to be preferred to an ungodly peace: no, in such cases, Christian princes are not only to be resisted unto, but not to be prayed for. For prayer must come of faith, and it is revealed to their consciences, that God will hear no prayer for such a prince. Judge then, Christian reader, if I wrong this sort of people, in giving them the style of that sect, whose errors they imitate: and since they are contented to wear their livery, let them not be ashamed to borrow also their name. It is only of this kind of men, that in this book I write so sharply; and whom I wish my son to punish, in case they refuse to obey the law, and will not cease to stir up a rebellion, whom against I have written the more bitterly, in respect of divers famous libels, and injurious speeches spread by some of them, not only dishonorably invective against all Christian princes, but even reproachful to our profession and religion, in respect they are come out under color thereof: and yet were never answered but by Papists, who generally meddle as well against them, as the religion itself: whereby the scandal was rather doubled, than taken away. But on the other part, I protest upon mine honor, I mean it not generally of all preachers, or others, that likes better of the single form of policy in our church, than of the many ceremonies in the Church of England; that are persuaded, that their bishops smell of a papal supremacy, that the surplice, the cornered cap, and such like are the outward badges of Popeish errors. No, I am so far from being contentious in these things—which for my own part I ever esteemed as indifferent—as I do equally love and honor the learned and grave men of either of these opinions. It can nowise become me to pronounce so lightly a

---

[328]**sit ... publicanus** *you are like a heathen and a publican* a reference to Mat 18:17 "And if he wil not vouchsafe to heare then, tel it unto the Church: and if he refuse to heare the Church also, let him be unto thee as a heathen man, and a Publicane."

sentence, in so older a controversy. We will (God be praised) do agree in the grounds, and the bitterness of men upon such questions, doth but trouble the peace of the church; and gives advantage and entry to the Papists by our division, that were the law is otherwise, they may content themselves soberly and quietly with their own opinions, no resisting to the authority, nor breaking the law of the country; neither above all, stirring any rebellion or schism: but possessing their souls in peace, let them preasse by patience, and well grounded reasons, either to persuade all the rest to like their judgments; or where they see better grounds on the other part, not to be ashamed peaceably to incline thereunto, laying aside all preoccupied opinions.

And that this is the only meaning of my book, and not any coldness or crack in religion, that place does plainly witness, whereafter I have spoken of the faults in our ecclesiastical estate, I exhort my son to be beneficial unto the good men of the ministry; praising God there, that there is presently a sufficient number of good men of them in this kingdom: and yet are they all known to be against the form of the English church. Yea, so far I am in that place from admitting corruption in Religion, as I wish him in promoting them, to use such caution, as may preserve their estate from creeping to corruption; ever using that form through the whole book, ever I speak of bad preachers, terming them some of the ministers, and not ministers or ministry in general. And to conclude this point of religion, what indifference of religion can *Momus* call that in me, where, speaking of my son's marriage (in case it pleased God before that time to cut the thread of my life) I plainly forewarn him of the inconvenience that were like to ensue in case he should marry any that be of a different profession in religion from him: notwithstanding that the number of princes professing our religion be so small, as it is hard to foresee, how he can be that way, meetlie[329] matched according to his rank.

And as for the other point, that by some parts in this

---

[329]**meetlie** fairly, appropriately

book, it should appear, that I do nourish in my mind, a vindictive resolution against England, or some principals there; it is surely more than wonderful unto me, upon what grounds they can have gathered such conclusions. For as upon the one part, I neither by name nor description point out England in that part of my discourse so upon the other, I plainly betray my meaning to be of Scotsmen, where I conclude that purpose in these terms: that the love I bear to my son, hath moved me to be so plain in this argument: for so that I discharge my conscience to him in uttering the verity, I care not what any traitor or treason-allower do think of it. And Englishmen could not thereby be meant, since they could be no traitors, where they ought no allegiance. I am not ignorant of a wise and princely apothegm, which the same Queen of England uttered about the time of her own coronation. But the drift of that discourse doth fully clear my intention, being only grounded upon that precept to my son, that he should not permit any unreverent detracting of his predecessors; bringing in that purpose of my mother only for an example of my experience anent Scotsmen, without using any persuasion to him of revenge. For a king's giving of any fault the due style, insures no reduction of the faulter's[330] pardon. No, I am be a degree nearer of kin unto my mother than he is, neither think I myself, either that unworthy, or that near my end, that I need to make such a Davidical testament;[331] since I have ever thought it the duty of a worthy prince, rather with a pike, than a pen, to write his just revenge. But in this matter I have no delight to be large, wishing all men to judge of my future projects, according to my bypast actions.

Thus having as much insisted in the clearing of these two points, as will (I hope) give sufficient satisfaction to all honest men, and leaving the envious to the food of their own venom;

---

[330]**faulter** wrongdoer
[331]1Kings 2:1–11, In which the dying David gives Solomon names of allies to reward and enemies to be eliminated.

TO THE READER

I will hartly pray thee, loving reader, charitably to conceive of my honest intention in this book. I know the greatest part of the people of this whole isle, have been very curious for a fight thereof: some for the love they bear me, either being particularly acquainted with me, or by a good report that perhaps they have heard of me and therefore longed to see any thing, that proceeded from that author whom they so loved and honored; since books are vive ideas of the author's mind. Some only for mere curiosity, that thinks it their honor to know all new things, were curious to glut their eyes therewith, only that they might vaunt them to have seen it: and some fraught with causeless envy at the author, did greedily search out the book thinking their stomach fit enough, for turning never so wholesome food in noisome and infective humors. So as this their great concurrence in curiosity (though proceeding from far different complexions) hath enforced the untimely divulging of this book, far contrary to my intention, as I have already said. To which hydra of diversely inclined spectators, I have no targe[332] to oppose but plainness, patience, and sincerity: plainness, for resolving and satisfying of the first sort: patience, for to bear with the shallowness of the next; and sincerity to defy the malice of the third withal. Though I cannot please all men therein, I am contented so that I only please the virtuous sort: and though they also find not every thing therein, so fully to answer their expectation, as the argument would seem to require; although I would wish them modestly to remember, that God has not bestowed all his gifts upon one, but parted them by a justice distributive; and that many eyes see more than one; and that the variety of men's minds is such, that *tot capita tot sensus*;[333] yea and that even the very faces, that God hath by nature brought forth in the world, do every one in some of their particular lineaments, differ from

---

[332]**targe** a type of traditional small Scots shield
[333]**tot...sensus** As *many heads, so many opinions.* Terence, *Phormio* (misquoted)

any other: yet in truth it was not my intention in handling of this purpose (as it is easy to perceive) fully to set down here all such grounds, as might out of the best writers have been alleged, out of my own invention and experience added, for the perfite institution of a king: but only to give some such precepts to my own son, for the government of this kingdom, as was meetest for him to be instructed in, and best became me to be the informer of.

If I in this book have been too particularly plain, impute it to the necessity of the subject, not so much being ordained for the institution of a prince in general, as I have said, as containing particular precepts to my son in special: whereof he could have made but a general use, if they had not contained the particular diseases of this kingdom, with the best remedies for the same; which it became me best as a king, having learned both the theoricke and practick thereof, more plainly to express, than any simple schoolman, that only knows matters of kingdoms by contemplation.

But if in some places it seems too obscure, impute it to the shortness thereof, being both for the respect of myself, and of my son, constrained thereunto: my own respect, for fault of leisure, being so continually occupied in the affairs of my office, as my great burden, and restless fashery[334] is more than known, to all that knows or hears of me: for my son's respect, because I know by myself, that a prince so long as he is young, will be so carried away with some sort of delight or other, that he cannot patiently abide the reading of any large volume: and when he comes to a full maturity of age, he must be so busied in the active part of his charge, a he will not be permitted to bestow many hours upon the contemplative part thereof. So as it was neither fit for him, nor possible for me, to have made this treatise any more ample than it is. Indeed I am little beholden to the curiosity of some, who thinking it too large already (as appears) for lack of leisure to copy it, drew some

---

[334]**fashery** worry

notes out of it, for speed's sake; putting in the one half of the purpose, and leaving out the other: not unlike the man that alleged that part of the psalm, *non est Deus*; but left out the preceding words, *Dixit insipiens in corde suo*.[335] And of these notes, making a little pamphlet (lacking both my method and half my matter) entitled it, forsooth, the *King's Testament*: as if I had eiked a third testament of my own, to the two that are in the Holy Scriptures. It is true that in a place thereof, for affirmation of the purpose I am speaking of to my son, I bring myself in there, as speaking upon my testament: for in that sense, every record in writing of a man's opinion in any thing (in respect that papers outlive their authors) is as it were a testament of that man's will in that case: and in that sense it is, that in that place I call this treatise a testament. But from any particular sentence in a book, to give the book itself a title, is as ridiculous, as to stile the book of the Psalms, the book of *Dixit insipiens*,[336] because with these words one of them doth begin.

Well, leaving these new paptizers and blockers of other men's books, to their own follies, I return to my purpose, anent the shortness of this book: suspecting that all my excuses for the shortness thereof, shall not satisfy some, especially in our neighbor country, who thought, that as I have so narrowly in this treatise touched all the principal sicknesses in our kingdom, with overtures for the remedies thereof, as I said before: so looked they to have found something therein, that should have touched the sicknesses of their state, in the like sort. But they will easily excuse me thereof, if they will consider the form I have used in this treatise; wherein I only teach my son, out of my own experience, what form of government is fittest for this kingdom: and in one part thereof speaking of the borders, I plainly there do excuse myself, that I will speak nothing of the state of England, as a matter wherein I never

---

[335]Ps 14:1 "The foole hathe said in his heart, There is no God..."
[336]**Dixit insipiens**[*The*] *fool says* The traditional Latin name for Psalm 14.

had experience. I know, indeed, no kingdom lacks her own diseases, and likewise that interest I have in the prosperity of that state: for although I would be silent, my blood and descent doth sufficiently proclaim it. But notwithstanding, since there is a lawful queen there presently reigning, who hath so long with so great wisdom and felicity governed her kingdoms, as (I must in true sincerity confess) the like hath not been read not heard of, either in our time, or since the days of the Roman Emperor Augustus, it could no wise become me, far inferior to her in knowledge and experience, to be a busybody in other prince's matters, and to fish in other folks' waters, as the proverb is. No, I hope by the contrary (with God's grace) ever to keep that Christian rule, to do as I would be done to: and I doubt nothing, yea even in her name I dare promise, by the bypast experience of her happy government, as I have already said, that no good subject shall be more careful to inform her of any corruptions stolen in her state; than she shall be zealous for the discharge of her conscience and honor, to see the same purged, and restored to the ancient integrity: and further, during her time, becomes me least of any to meddle in.

And thus having resolved all the doubts, so far as I can imagine, may be moved against this treatise; it only rests to pray thee (charitable reader) to interpret favorably this birth of mine, according to the integrity of the author, and not looking for perfection in the work itself. As for my part, I only glory thereof in this point, that I trust no sort of virtue in condemned nor any degree of vice allowed in it: and that (though it be not perhaps so gorgeously decked, and richly attired as it ought to be) it is at the least rightly proportioned in all the members, without any monstrous deformity in any of them: and specially that since it was first written in secret, and is now published, not of ambition, but of a kind of necessity; it must be taken of all men, for the true image of my very mind, and form of the rule, which I have prescribed to myself and mine. Which as in all my actions I have hitherto preassed to express, so far as the nature of my charge, and the condition of time would permit me, so bear it a discovery of that, which may be looked for at my hand, and whereto, even in my secret thoughts, I have engaged my self for the time to come. And thus in a firm trust, that it shall please God, who with my being and crown, gave me this mind, to maintain and augment the same in me, and my posterity, to the discharge of our conscience, the maintenance of our honor, and weal of our people, I bid thee hartly farewell.

Glossary

ado *going on; afoot*
allie *alliance*
anent *regarding, about*
arbitral *of or pertaining to arbiters; subject to the exercise of will*
archi-bellowces *large bellows*
arles-pennie *earnest money; a pledge to seal a bargain*
auditoure *audience*
aver *cart horse*
aye *always; still*

bairdes *poets (bards); mockers or lampooners*
bairnes *children*
balladines *dancers*
baloppes *codpiece*
be-gesse *at a guess, at random*
begouth *began*
boggle *shadow, goblin, specter*
brook *use or enjoy*
burreaux *hangmen*
bursten *burst; overpowered*

caitche *a type of handball game that was popular in James' Scottish court*
Candie *(1) the city of Candia (modern Heraklion) in Crete (2) Crete, in general*
choppes *strikes, attacks rudely, or flogs*

clouts *clothing*

cogging *drinking. A cog was a small wooden bowl or cup used to hold liquor.*

coinzie *coin*

compeere *present one's self in court after being summoned*

counte book *account book*

craiges *necks or throats*

crak *talk, converse*

cranne-craige *crane's neck*

curious *skillful, fastidious, particular*

dantone *subdue or tame*

declarator *a formal judicial declaration of a particular fact or legal right*

delate *explain or discourse at length*

delatoures *accusers*

dependers *followers, dependents*

dictone *dictum*

difficile *difficult*

dilated person *the person reported on*

dispone *revise legally*

dited *dictated, written*

ditement *something indited or dictated by another*

doazen *benumb, stupefy*

eike *add, augment, or increase*

empyring *governing, umpiring*

engine *genius, wit, disposition*

enregistrate *recorded*

fain of *happy enough with*

fairding *painting, disguising*

faschious *troublesome*

fashery *worry*

faulter *wrongdoer*

floures *decorations, flourishes (lit.* flowers)

fonde *silly, stupid, unprofitable*

GLOSSARY

forefaltures *judiciary forfeitures of property*
fra *from the time*
freats *superstitious notions, premonitions*

gage *to pledge or wager*
galliardest *sprightly, brisk, lively*
garre *cause or force*
gaygeour *a wager*
gazingly *intently*
glaikerie *folly, caprice*
glistering *glittering, shining*
gust *taste*
gysares *maskers or harlequins*

habilitie *ability; physical strength*
happe *good luck*
hartlinesse *cordiality, warmth of heart*
haunt *frequent; stay near*
homely *informal; plain spoken*
hornes *legal procedures in which a defendant was denounced as a rebel or traitor in the Scots courts*

intromission *legal term for act of meddling with another's property*
inwardest *most intimate*

Janissairs *Janissaries*
jowking *bending down the body with a quick motion*

kithe *to show, make known by one's actions*

law-borrows *legal security posted by one person that he will not do personal or property injury to another*
leid *song, lay*
Lentron *Lent*
lighlying *underestimating, speaking lightly of*
lippening *trusting*
liverentars *tenants*

lowable *laudable, commendable*
lugg *ear*

manyest *majority*
marrowes *mates, companions*
meaned *lamented*
meetlie *fairly, appropriately*
mell *involve oneself with*
middes *middle or average*
middeses *means*
mignarde *delicate; effeminate*
mint *try, attempt*
misnurtured *ill bred*
morgue *a strange, solemn face*
mowes *mocks or jests*
moyen *property, means*

nourish-father *nurturing father*
nourish-milk *nurse's milk*

or *ere, before*
orping *fretting, repining*
over-homely *overly familiar*

painful *painstaking*
panse *consider or meditate on*
pare nails *trim (finger) nails*
passe-master *a craftsman who has passed the examination for master's rank*
pensel *a small streamer or flag*
perfite *perfect, skillful or complete*
perte *brisk, lively, smart*
pose *a hoard or hidden treasure*
powle hair *cut hair*
preasse *attempt*
preined *decked, trimmed*

rathest *fastest; most savagely*

GLOSSARY

reik *smoke*

ripely advise *give sufficient consideration*

rumling *noisy, rambunctious*

sensyne *since then*

sibbe *kindred; nearly related; like*

smoared down *smothered, suffocated*

snapper out well grossly *be quick to find big faults*

snibbe sickerlie *check, hinder, reproach*

spie *observe*

sporters *companions in leisure activities*

syne *afterwards, later*

taking narrow tente *observing carefully*

taking the pet *taking offense, being in a bad humor*

targe *a type of traditional small Scots shield*

textuary *one who is knowledgeable about sacred texts*

theoricke *theory*

thereanents *thereabouts*

therethrough *thereby*

thrall *enslave*

thralldom *slavery, bondage*

thraw *twist, wrench, wreathe, cast, or throw*

tigging *touching lightly, dallying with*

timously *in good time*

tinsell *loss*

tome *drawn out*

toyes *toys; idle or speculative thoughts*

tratler *tattler, prattler*

trow *believe*

truchmen *interpreters, translators*

underogating *not detracting from*

unspeered at *unspoken to*

vague *stray*

vaik *become vacant*

vive *alive; vivid; lively*

walkerise *watchful*
weill *benefit, advantage*
wight *creator, maker*
wrak *ruin*

Index

INDEX

Bibliography

The following were used by the editor in preparing the front matter and annotations. Works marked with an asterisk were either directly referenced by James in the text, or there is other reason to believe that he had access to them (though generally not in the specific edition listed). Reprinted works list the original publication date in parentheses if known.

*Aesop. *Aesop's Fables, Embellished with One Hundred and Eleven Emblematical Devices.* Project Gutenberg. (1814) 2012.

Alíghíerí, Dante. *The Divine Comedy.* Bergin, T. G. (trans.) Appleton-Century-Crofts. 1955.

"Authorized Version" in *The Catholic Encyclopedia: A Machine Readable Edition.* University of Oxford Text Archive. (1907–1917) 1996.

Ballou, Maturin M. *Pearls of Thought.* Project Gutenberg. (1880) 2008.

Bell, Henry Glassford. *Life of Mary Queen of Scots.* Project Gutenberg. (1828) 2011.

Bennett, Charles E. *New Latin Grammar.* Project Gutenberg. (1918) 2005.

Bible. Geneva Version. Geneva: 1560.

Bible. Latin Vulgate Version.

Bible. New Revised Standard Version. Thomas Nelson. 1990.

Brown, Sangor II. *The Sex Worship and Symbolism of Primitive Races: An Interpretation.* Project Gutenberg. (1916) 2009.

Cato, Dionysys. *Disticha Catonis.* The Latin Library. http://www.thelatinlibrary.com/cato.dis.html

Chaucer, Geoffrey. *Chaucer's Works. Volume 6: Introduction, Glossary, and Indexes.* W. Skeat (ed.) Project Gutenberg. (1846) 2013.

Conti, Brooke. *Confessions of Faith in Early Modern England.* University of Pennsylvania Press. 2014.

Conway, Moncure Daniel. *Solomon and Solomonic Literature.* Project Gutenberg. (1899) 2012.

*Cicero, Marcus Tullius. *Cicero's Tusculun Disputations; Also, Treatises on the Nature of the Gods, and on The Commonwealth.* Project Gutenberg. (1877) 2005.

——*Delphi Complete Works of Cicero.* 2014.

*Dio, Cassius. *Dio's Rome.* Foster, H. B. (trans.) Project Gutenberg. (1906) 2004.

Durant, Will. *The Age of Reason Begins.* Simon & Schuster. 1961.

—— *Caesar and Christ.* Simon & Schuster. 1944.

—— *The Reformation.* Simon & Schuster. 1957.

—— *The Story of Philosophy.* Simon & Schuster. 1933.

Ffoulkes, Charles John. *Armour & Weapons.* Project Gutenberg. (1909) 2012.

Gardner, J. Starkie & Farquharson, V. A. *Armour in England.* Project Gutenberg. (1897) 2013.

Hallam, Henry. *The constitutional history of England: from the accession of Henry VII to the death of George II.* Wells and Lilly. 1829.

Hobbes, Thomas. *Leviathan.* Project Gutenberg. (1651) 2009.

*Horace, *The Art of Poetry: An Epistle to the Pisos.* Colmon, G. (trans) Project Gutenberg. (1783) 2005.

Howie, John. *Biographia Scoticana (Scots Worthies).* Project Gutenberg. (1781) 2009.

BIBLIOGRAPHY

"James I" in *Encyclopaedia Brittanica.* 11th ed.

Jamieson's Dictionary of the Scottish Language. J. Longmuir (ed.) William P. Nimmo. 1867.

Josephus, Flavius. *Antiquities of the Jews.* Project Gutenberg. William Whiston (trans.) 2013.

Lang, Andrew. *The Mystery of Mary Stuart.* Project Gutenberg. (1901) 2013.

—— *A Short History of Scotland.* Project Gutenberg. (1911) 2005.

*Laërtius, Diogenes. *Lives of the Eminent Philosophers.* Hicks, R. D. (trans.) University of Adelaide Library. 2014.

"Lipsius, Justus" in *Encyclopaedia Brittanica.* 11th ed.

Marsh, Christopher W. *The Family of Love in English Society 1550–1630.* Cambridge University Press. 1994.

Marshall, John. *John Locke: Resistance, Religion, and Responsibility.* Cambridge University Press. 1994.

Michison, Rosalind. *The History of Scotland* rev. ed. Routledge. 2002.

Murray, Margaret A. *The Witch-Cult in Western Europe: A Study in Anthropology.* Project Gutenberg. (1921) 2007.

Oliphant, Margaret. *Royal Edinburgh: Her Saints, Kings, Prophets, and Poets.* Project Gutenberg. (1891) 2008.

Onions, C. T. & Eagleson, R. D. *A Shakespeare Glossary.* Oxford University Press. 1985.

Patton, Francis L. *Presbyterian Principles: A Discourse.* Metropolitan Printing Co. 1875.

*Plutarch. Moralia. Loeb Classical Library. 1936.

——*Plutarch's Lives.* A. H. Clough (trans.) Project Gutenberg. 1996.

Rabelais, François. *Gargantua and Pantagruel.* Urquhart, T. & Motteux, P.A. (trans.) Project Gutenberg. (1894) 2004.

Rebhorn, Wayne A. "Introduction" in *The Prince and Other Writings*. Barnes & Noble Classics. 2003.

Rees, Abraham. *The Cyclopaedia; Or, Universal Dictionary of Arts, Sciences and Literature*. Volume 18. Longman, Hurst. 1819.

Roberts, Alexander. *A Treatise on Witchcraft*. Project Gutenberg. (1616) 2005.

Shakespeare, William. *The Riverside Shakespeare*. Houghton Mifflin. 1974.

*Siculus, Diodorus. *The Library of History*. Loeb Classical Library. 1954.

Simpson, D. P. *Cassell's Latin Dictionary*. Macmillan. (1968) 1977.

Skouen, Tina. *The Value of Time in Early Modern English Literature*. Routledge. 2017.

"Smith, Young, and Sgrymgeour Mss." *Notes and Quearies*. No. 188, June 4, 1853. Project Gutenberg. 2007.

Spottiswood, Robert. *Practicks of the Law of Scotland*. 1706.

*Suetonius, Tranquilus. *The Lives of the Twelve Caesars*. Thompson, A. (trans.) Project Gutenberg. 2004.

Toynbee, Arnold J. *A Study of History (Abridgment of Volumes I–VI)*. Sommerville, D. C. (ed.) Oxford University Press. 1947.

Tyndale, William.*W.T. Pentateuch 1530–37 and N.T. 1525–26*. Project Gutenberg. 2004.

Wallace, Robert & J. C. Smith. *George Buchanan*. Project Gutenberg. (1899) 2014.

Wood, William. *Elizabethan Sea Dogs*. Project Gutenberg. (1918) 2004.

*Xenophon. *Cyropaedia: The Education of Cyrus*. Daykyns, H. G. (trans). Project Gutenberg. 2009.

——* *The Symposium*. Daykyns, H.G. (trans.) Project Gutenberg. 2008.

About the Editor

Kevin A. Straight lives in Los Angeles County, California with his partner, a cat, and a turtle. He has previously published short stories and an academic monograph and has been blogging since 2008. Kevin also hosts a streaming television show, *Handyman Kevin*, on YouTube in which he teaches ordinary people how to be master handy-people.

Kevin holds an MBA degree from the University of California, Riverside and undergraduate degrees from Western Governors University and Flathead Valley Community College, and suspects that his educational journey is far from over.

For news about Kevin and his upcoming projects, please visit http://www.kevinastraight.com.